Praise for Seen and (

Jill has been an active member of our church family for years, and in that time she has become a good friend. Jill's writing has always been exceptional. Her work on *Seen and Invited* simply demonstrates her at her best. In *Seen and Invited* Jill combines poetic artistry with thorough, in-depth study into both the Gospels and their cultural setting. Yet she does more! She adds a third aspect of her own personal self-reflection and vulnerability to these essays. And as a result, they truly come to life in a fresh, artistic and yet very personal, relatable way!

---Rev. Rick Durrance, Rector, Wilmore Anglican Church

If you've ever traveled the road of brokenness, complete with potholes and dangerous curves of isolation, unworthiness, shame, and hopelessness, Jill Penrod's *Seen and Invited* is a special gift. Travel along a few dusty roads with Jesus as he heals the sick (physically and spiritually), repairs the broken, restores the outcasts, touches the untouchables, and extends much-needed grace and forgiveness to the lost and forgotten. Jill Penrod's unique and masterful storytelling will leave you wanting more. By the end of the book, you will be asking Jesus to be *Seen and Invited*. Highly recommended.

---Therese Kilgore, Retired, Licensed Professional Counselor

I have known Jesus since I was a little girl and served him in healthcare for 30 years (3 in seminary), but I saw the Lord anew reading Jill's excellent book. She digs deep into his encounters with people on the roads of brokenness, doubt, discontentment, isolation and insignificance. Jill shows us how Jesus invites us to a life of wholeness and purpose. And her historical knowledge gave deeper understanding to many familiar stories. Now I'm inspired to help others be seen and invited by Jesus!

---Karen Hussar, retired Occupational Therapist

Seen and Invited

MEETING JESUS ON THE DUSTY ROADS

JILL PENROD

Published by Jill Penrod/Lamp Oil Resources
Copyright 2024
All Rights Reserved

Scripture quotations marked (NLT) are taken from the *Holy Bible*, New Living Translation, copyright ©1996, 2004, 2015 by Tyndale House Foundation. Used by permission of Tyndale House Publishers, Carol Stream, Illinois 60188. All rights reserved.

Scripture quotations marked ESV are from the ESV® Bible (The Holy Bible, English Standard Version®), © 2001 by Crossway, a publishing ministry of Good News Publishers. Used by permission. All rights reserved. The ESV text may not be quoted in any publication made available to the public by a Creative Commons license. The ESV may not be translated in whole or in part into any other language.

Scripture marked International Children's Bible is from The Holy Bible, International Children's Bible® Copyright© 1986, 1988, 1999, 2015 by Thomas Nelson. Used by permission.

Revised Standard Version of the Bible, copyright © 1946, 1952, and 1971 the Division of Christian Education of the National Council of the Churches of Christ in the United States of America. Used by permission. All rights reserved.

Tree of Life (TLV) Translation of the Bible. Copyright © 2015 by The Messianic Jewish Family Bible Society.

All unmarked Scripture quotations are taken from the Holy Bible, New International Version®, NIV®. Copyright ©1973, 1978, 1984, 2011 by Biblica, Inc.™ Used by permission of Zondervan. All rights reserved worldwide. www.zondervan.com The "NIV" and "New International Version" are trademarks registered in the United States Patent and Trademark Office by Biblica, Inc.™

Table of Contents

Table of Contents 5

The Journey Begins 7

Section One: The Pitted Road of Brokenness 13
    Proximity Matters 14
    Do You Want to Get Well? 23
    The Touch of the Shepherd's Hand 33
    True Wholeness 42

Section Two: The Dark Road of Doubt (and Fear!) 50
    Sunk by Doubt 51
    I Do Believe 62
    An Incomplete Faith 72

Section Three: The Twisting Road of Discontentment 82
    In Need of a Drink 84
    Filled Baskets and Mother Love 96
    Delighted by Understanding 106

Section Four: The Silent Road of Isolation 116
    No Strength of Her Own 118
    When the Crowd Won't Forgive 126
    Restoration after a Fall 134

Section Five: The Flat Road of Insignificance 144
    Come and See 146
    Gone Fishin' 157
    Clean Feet 165

Into the Future.. 176
Study Guide.. 178
Notes.. 191
   The Voices of Jill Penrod... 195

The Journey Begins...

I have always been a King David fangirl. Yes, David from the Bible, the shepherd-turned-king. I mean, the guy is larger than life. He lived and wrote with such passion for God, passion for living in general. One day in heaven, I want to dance with David, the kind of wild, I-love-God-with-no-reservations dancing that caused David's wife to turn from him in embarrassment.

David's psalms are my happy place. I've read them dozens of times, studied them, journaled about most of them. So, when God placed the desire in my heart to add nonfiction writing to my repertoire (I'm a fiction writer by trade), I knew without a doubt I would be writing about David, specifically the Psalms of David.

Except I was wrong. During Epiphany of 2023, my pastor said something during a sermon that caught my attention. Why, he asked, did the disciples accept Jesus's call to follow him? At that point he had done no miracles. He'd barely started teaching. What caused these men to drop everything and follow a young, untried rabbi wandering around the Sea of Galilee?

I'm not sure why the question niggled like it did. I honestly don't remember one other word of that sermon, so I don't remember what answer the pastor gave. What I do know is that within a few days I had an answer. Jesus drew people because he saw them deeply and invited them into a bigger story.

This may not sound like a grand revelation. However, it was epic for me, because, as much as I fangirled over David, able to imagine his personality, poring over his stories and his songs, I kept distance from Jesus. Jesus had always been a little fuzzy to me.

Did I love him? Sure, he died for me. What's not to love?

But maybe... No. Well, yes and no. I wanted to love with David's love, filled with passion and emotion, but I wasn't quite there. Belief, faith, honor, respect? Yes. But not dance-half-naked-in-the-streets joy and love.

If you asked me to sum up Jesus in one word, it would be *exasperated*. This man wandered Judea asking people where their faith was. Why were they afraid? I heard it as *What is wrong with you people?* It didn't feel like love. I knew it was and wanted it to be, but I hadn't quite gotten there.

As I pondered why my pastor's few words hit like they did, God took me back to the beginning, back to that moment I decided I wanted Jesus in my life.

The moment is clear. I was very young. Six? Eight? I was sitting on my bed with this little box of booklets about Jesus. One was pink. Another purple. I looked at them all the time, because I loved books, and I loved to read, and something about these little books called to me.

In one of them—maybe the pink one—the writer mentioned that Jesus wanted to be my friend. I don't remember much about that little girl on the bed. She could be too big for her britches. She was an overthinker, too anxious, and didn't do that well with people. People weren't knocking down the door to be her friend. (Oh, I'd love to say those things changed, but alas…)

To that little girl, the idea that Jesus wanted to be her friend was amazing. Very soon after that I was baptized and joined my church.

Jump ahead a few years, and somehow the wisdom of that little girl had been lost. Some of it had to do with my faith community. My church wasn't bad, but obedience was a little more important than love. God's wrath was a little more important than God's grace.

Some of it had to do with those tragic moments in every life when God feels far away, when evil seems to win. Instead of clinging to Jesus when those moments came, I built a wall against him and the pain of this world.

Through it all, I lost track of Jesus as my friend and began to see him as the frustrated man who might not want me around because I exasperated him.

I'd love to say this problem was quickly resolved. The truth is I've waffled over Jesus for a long time, wanting that King David, trust-God-with-everything love, wanting the comfort that little girl found in Jesus as a friend. But too often my heart heard the Sermon on the Mount and forgot the healings in the streets. Sometimes, it seems, we have to walk mighty far into the desert before we find the path back.

During Epiphany 2023, I started the path home.

Called home

So, back to the story. I had this revelation. Seen and invited.
Seen. And *Invited*.

I'm an introvert by nature. And, forgive the arrogance in this statement, I am an intelligent introvert. I learn fast. I understand things. I have insights and see patterns.

But the introvert trumps the smart girl, and I live invisibly. Not many people have heard my insights. Not many people look me in the eye and dig in, because the introvert likes to hide, and only with some searching can the smart girl be found. Very few people have looked for her, and she's kind of dying to get out.

But Jesus sees. He looks deeply, and he sees. The friend that little girl longed for on her bed with her pink book? Jesus saw her, too. In just a few moments, I was back there. Things that had been fuzzy for years were clearing up. *Jesus sees me. He's looking for me and finds me.*

And invited? Wow. Remember in gym class when teams were chosen? Remember that girl or boy who was always, without fail, chosen last? Yeah, that was me. I didn't get invited very often. Because of that anxious introvert I wear on the surface and that smart girl who's sometimes too big for her britches I carry inside, I don't have a lifetime of grand invitations.

But Jesus sees deeper than what I show, and he invites me into an adventure I don't feel worthy of undertaking. He calls me to dance along the road in joy like David and do the unthinkable for him.

It's breathtaking.

Meeting the Shepherd

Still, how to get past exasperated Jesus? I want to be seen. I want to be invited. But years of seeing Jesus with the wrong eyes isn't that easy to ignore.

One thing I love about David is all the talk of him being a shepherd. The shepherd imagery speaks to my deepest soul. I'm a mom of four, took care of a household, and taught my kids from home. I had varying degrees of success at these endeavors, and sometimes the weight of the world seemed to rest on my shoulders.

The idea of being a silly lamb leaping around without a care, having someone strong and kind and gentle scoop me up and carry me out of brambles and put me on his shoulders as we slosh through deep water... Yeah. I want to be tended like a lamb. It sounds delightful. Green pastures. Still waters. Restored soul.

But Jesus is exasperated. I'm not holy enough. I'm not faithful enough. God wants obedience, right? Jesus killed a fig tree for not having fruit. What if I don't have enough fruit?

At this point I felt the powerful pull to write a Bible study about Jesus seeing and inviting people. I wasn't sure about this, because I hadn't figured Jesus out yet, but the seed was there. He loved me, saw me, and invited me. That called to my weary heart like you wouldn't believe.

He was the shepherd. He said so himself. But what about the exasperated part? What about the sermons about being holy, when I feel like a mess? If Jesus sees me and invites me, will he really want to keep me?

This is where another God-given love in my life came into play. I love history. I minored in history in college completely by accident, using all my elective hours to take history courses until I realized I'd completed a minor. And yet, I knew nothing of Jesus in terms of history.

That was the leg of the journey where it all fell into place. I began to study how Jesus taught, how he acted, why he did what he did in light of the historical context of Israel at that time. What was a rabbi? Why did he talk in parables? What about his use of hyperbole and Old Testament scripture?

If you're not a historian, don't worry. All that was simply a means to get me from point A to point B, and God wanted me at point B. Yes, you have to hear a little about history in the pages ahead, but it won't hurt or take over. I promise. But oh, for the history buff inside me… Some scales fell off my eyes, and it all made sense. The different aspects of Jesus came together, and the little girl found her friend again.

I realized Jesus performed the most amazing balancing act while he was here. The Old Testament speaks of him as a prophet, so he did a lot of prophet-like things, some of which made him sound exasperated. He came as a king, so he wielded a lot of authority. Again, not entirely personal.

But the Old Testament also points to Jesus as a shepherd. God sent a lot of kings to Israel. He sent a lot of prophets. The kings varied, some good and some bad. The prophets were rather disliked, never saying what people wanted to hear.

But the shepherd… There were two. Funny that I fangirled over the first, David the king, and nearly missed the second, Jesus the Messiah.

What I missed was that Jesus loved being the shepherd. Prophets don't draw adoring crowds of thousands. Shepherds do. Caretakers can. Jesus drew a tired and oppressed people through his shepherding, tending each soul. He interacted with the people one by one on the dusty roads, village by village, broken person by broken person.

And I hadn't paid attention. I saw healing and miracles as signs of who Jesus was and not what he loved.

I missed that healing and miracles and interacting and walking those roads—that's what separated him from every prophet, every king, even David the shepherd king, who had to lead a nation. Jesus delights in the dusty roads.

Jesus delights in meeting people on those roads and gently guiding them to the better road, the safer, cleaner, straighter, solid road to his eternal kingdom. He *delights* in it. He never stood up and told the crowd he was a prophet or a king. He called himself a shepherd. That was his love.

That was the moment this book was born. That was the beginning of my journey down the dusty roads of Israel, and now I invite you—wherever you are, whoever you are—to come walk with me. Meet the lost, the broken, the confused, the angry… Meet the lambs. Watch Jesus gather them in his arms in a way nobody ever had before.

I can fangirl over David all I want, but he's finished. He's dead and buried, not much more than a story.

But when I started walking down the dusty roads with Jesus, roads of brokenness, doubt, discontent, loneliness, and insignificance, and I watched him lead people to the road of wholeness, trust, fulfillment, belonging, and purpose, I found something so much deeper.

I left my dead shepherd crush behind, and I fell in love with the shepherd who's never going anywhere. I found my friend. Yes, he's a prophet and a king, the savior of the world, but when I grow weary, it's the shepherd and friend who puts me on his shoulders and sloshes through the mud with me.

Join me on the dusty roads. Let's meet Jesus's deepest heart and pet a few beloved lambs along the way.

Section One: The Pitted Road of Brokenness

The road of brokenness. If you've walked this world for any length of time, you've been there. It's pitted and cracked, and those who walk it trip over their pasts and their pain. The road looks like the people who walk on it: damaged, twisted, and worn.

Jesus found a whole lot of broken people during his time on earth. Many were physically broken. Most were broken at deeper levels, too. Jesus desires healthy sheep. He wants his lambs to thrive. Green pastures. Still waters. Restored souls. For many, that restoration begins with the healing of broken places.

For the rest of the book I plan to walk down a few roads, like this road of brokenness. Many of the stories would fit in more than one chapter. Jesus healed individuals. He didn't categorize us as the broken, the doubting, or the restless. All of those are levels of brokenness. All of those problems lead to isolation and doubt and make us wonder at our purpose. I lumped them so I'd appear to have some kind of organization, but each tale is its own.

So don't worry too much about which story is on which road. Somewhere in here you'll meet yourself. I almost guarantee it. Likely, you'll see a little of yourself in every story.

Jesus planned it that way. He was only here to touch people for a few years, and he needed to leave a legacy that would touch hundreds and thousands down through the ages. Everything he did and taught had to speak to hundreds of souls. You're on some dusty road somewhere. We're going to find you and let Jesus touch you and  restore you and give you a grand invitation, because you're never so lost and remote that you can't be found.

Proximity Matters

We start on this dusty road with a well-known story. In fact, most of the stories we'll unpack are familiar, children's stories told by most every Sunday school teacher. Miracles and healing are concrete and easier to explain to a child than the complex teachings of Jesus, so for many of us these stories are comfortable and known, like curling up in a worn chair with a mug of hot chocolate on a cold day. Remember, for me this journey started as a little girl, so feel free to invite your own inner little girl or little boy to read them with the wonder of a child.

But we're older now, more cynical, more worn. Don't worry, because Jesus came to a tired, worn people. When he came onto the scene, Israel had gone four hundred years without a prophet. No son of David was on the throne. Israel had lost her autonomy, her heritage, her hope. Spiritual leaders were as cynical as the people: Pharisees creating their thousands of traditions hoping to force God to send the Messiah; Sadducees who believed this tired life was all the life a person would have; even priests who didn't always wield their power with care.

Your older, tired, broken self is exactly who Jesus meant to find on the broken road, and he hoped to replace that tired soul with the joy, excitement, and faith of a child. So whichever self you bring to these stories, know Jesus will tenderly speak to you.

It begins with the tale of a man lowered through a roof.

When my youngest son was small, this was his favorite Bible story. What child doesn't love a story with some well-meaning vandalism? It's every child's dream. So we'll start here, because if we can't look at this situation with a smile, I think we miss something important, and Jesus loses a little dimension. I lived too long with a flat version of Jesus. Let's reinflate him back into a three-dimensional, fully human, fully divine soul who walked our roads and yet did it differently, better.

Luke tells our story this way:

Some men came carrying a paralyzed man on a mat and tried to take him into the house to lay him before Jesus. ¹⁹ When they could not find a way to do this because of the crowd, they went up on the roof and lowered him on his mat through the tiles into the middle of the crowd, right in front of Jesus.
²⁰ When Jesus saw their faith, he said, "Friend, your sins are forgiven."
²¹ The Pharisees and the teachers of the law began thinking to themselves, "Who is this fellow who speaks blasphemy? Who can forgive sins but God alone?"
²² Jesus knew what they were thinking and asked, "Why are you thinking these things in your hearts? ²³ Which is easier: to say, 'Your sins are forgiven,' or to say, 'Get up and walk'? ²⁴ But I want you to know that the Son of Man has authority on earth to forgive sins." So he said to the paralyzed man, "I tell you, get up, take your mat and go home." ²⁵ Immediately he stood up in front of them, took what he had been lying on and went home praising God. ²⁶ Everyone was amazed and gave praise to God. They were filled with awe and said, "We have seen remarkable things today." Luke 5:18-26

A Little Well-Meaning Vandalism

Let's start with the part that made your younger self smile. First, this is probably Peter's house. Mark tells us this happened in Capernaum, and that Jesus had *come home*. Matthew 8:14-16 takes place in Peter's home in Capernaum, and many scholars agree Jesus normally stayed with Peter when in Capernaum. If you don't know much about Peter, he tended to be the voice of the disciples. He was loyal, stood up for Jesus, and occasionally said bombastic things hoping to prove himself to Jesus. It wouldn't be a surprise that he offered his house when the group stayed in Capernaum.

So we have Peter's house filled to the brim with people. Mark 2:2 says it this way: *They gathered in such large numbers that there was no room left, not even outside the door, and he preached the word to them.* I wonder what Peter's wife thought about this. Or his mother-in-law, who likely shared this home, as well. The event must have been loud and chaotic, the air in the room tight and smelling of too many overwarm bodies. Maybe Peter waffled between pride at seeing his home used by his beloved rabbi and frustration, because a loud, dense crowd might not be careful of a person's possessions.

That all paled, though, when someone began to tear up the roof. I'm sure everyone realized this was happening. Recently our roof lost half its shingles in a windstorm, and when things happen on a roof, it's not quiet. If Jesus was teaching, the group might not have been moving much, and all eyes shifted up in surprise.

I wonder if the room got silent. Did Peter look at Jesus in wonder? Did he hope Jesus would stop this? It was his house, for crying out loud. Would Jesus let people tear up his house?

I can't help but imagine Peter's look of baffled frustration, followed by Jesus's reaction, which I imagine was a smile. Maybe more than a smile. Maybe Jesus bent over in a full belly laugh at the ingenuity of these men and Peter's waffling reaction. Jesus's ministry was still new. His disciples hadn't yet seen the full range of wonders, but at this moment they knew following Jesus was something unique.

So the crowd steps or scoots back to keep from being knocked down by a man lowered from the roof, and the man ends up on a mat at Jesus's feet.

Forgiven First

Here's where we move from the children's story to the adult version. When we see where this man ends up, we see something that will be a hallmark of Jesus's ministry from here to the end. Jesus healed people one by one. Those closest to him were given his attention, his care, and his miraculous invitations to wholeness and healing.

What these men had already learned from watching Jesus this short time was that proximity mattered.

I've thought about this a lot in my life. Jesus had three years to make such an impact on the world that we still talk about it and learn from it two thousand years later. Three years isn't long. He could have healed many, many more people if he'd walked to the entrance to each city, held up his hands, called a little thunder, and healed everyone in town in one sweep of his arms.

But that isn't how he did it. He looked at each individual person. Jesus's ministry as a shepherd required him to chase down and rescue each lamb from his or her own briar patch, his or her own crooked road, his or her own raging river.

Back to our man at Jesus's feet. Jesus had to look down to focus on him. Right now, I want you to look down. Your range of vision shifts, doesn't it? At the moment you can see very little, just what's on the floor below. The same happened here. For a moment, Jesus saw nothing but this man whose friends had broken all kinds of protocols of hospitality, torn up a roof, and dropped him here.

This man was loved by his friends. Jesus knew their desperation and their devotion, and his heart went out to them, to all of them.

He opens the conversation with this man speaking words that cause a stir, because Jesus was in the habit of causing a stir. Remember, he had three years. He couldn't blend into the crowd. He also couldn't blend into the crowd because he was the Son of God, the first and only Son of God to show up. Everything he did happened a little differently than expected.

His words might have disappointed the man on the mat as well as the men looking down from the roof, but now that we know the whole story, they are the most precious words in the world.

As Matthew puts it, *When Jesus saw their faith, he said to the man, "Take heart, son; your sins are forgiven."* Matthew 9:2b

They expected a healing. That's what they'd come for. They'd torn up a man's roof for it. Instead, Jesus grants forgiveness. Was Jesus able to do that? Was it real or just words? Those in the room had no way to know. Jesus was still new on the scene. Yes, his healing wasn't normal, but to take on the role of the priests, especially granting forgiveness to someone who didn't speak of repentance... This wasn't quite right.

The Pharisees in the room called Jesus on it. Yes, a priest could offer forgiveness to someone who came repenting and asking for it, but that hadn't happened here. They weren't exactly wrong to question a new rabbi who granted forgiveness like a priest.

Jesus has to look up. That moment between Jesus and the paralyzed man snaps, and the crowd comes back into focus. I wonder if Jesus was standing or seated in this scene. Had he squatted low to speak to the man? Had he touched him? He'd called him *son* and told him to take heart. For one brief moment the man thought this was it. He had the attention of the rabbi. He was here at his feet, as close as he could get. And yet, this hadn't gone as planned.

A Blood Promise

Jesus now speaks to the crowd. One thing to remember in our journey with Jesus is that he lived with an audience. And again, he had this limit of time. Everything he said and did was efficient and spoke to many people at many levels. This story is no different. He has a lesson for Peter as his house is dismantled—*Be patient, Peter. These lambs are the most important thing in the world to me. Let them come however they need to come.* He had a lesson for the men on the roof—*I see your friend. Your faith speaks to my heart, and I love this broken man as much and even more than you do.* And he has a message for the spiritual skeptics.

That message was that the authority to heal, which Israel hadn't seen in ages, spoke of deeper things. It spoke of Jesus's authority to forgive. I doubt any of them understood what that meant, what price Jesus would pay to buy that forgiveness. When he forgave that man, he spoke of something horrible in his own future. It wasn't a ritual of a priest, but instead a promise of blood and tears from Jesus's own life a few short years down the road.

Jesus promised that man the very blood in his veins. And nobody realized.

Jesus started with forgiveness to get their attention, to hear them grumble, to once again turn the expectations of the tired, frustrated, confused Israelites on their heads.

But he also started with forgiveness because that's the road to wholeness for the broken people on the road. Proximity to Jesus and rightness of relationship with Jesus—what's more important than that? Everything in our spiritual walk hinges on those two things. The man's friends helped with the first. Jesus himself offered the second.

Because nobody understood the promise in the words and the future agony they would require, and because Jesus loved this man and his friends and even the skeptics in the room, he follows up by doing what they hoped. Again he turns his attention to the man, and he orders him to get up, take his mat, and go home. He does, praising God all the way.

The crowd must have parted to let him out. His friends must have scrambled off the roof, laughing and hugging and dancing through the streets. Their friend was healed. Their rude risk had paid off.

The man was also forgiven. Jesus told him to take heart, to have courage. He called him son. Those moments when Jesus looked down into his face, maybe crouched at his side, when the crowd fell away and the rabbi gave him full attention—those moments would stay with that man forever. He would remember the Pharisees' complaint. He would remember Jesus saying he had the authority to forgive sins. A few years later, when this rabbi was killed and a new sect appeared speaking of his resurrection, this man would stop and listen.

I doubt the forgiveness part mattered for a while. Having a working body would take center stage. And that's okay. When Jesus finds a broken soul on the road, what he does might take time to process. He doesn't want to heal us in part. He wants us whole. True wholeness is about the entire person, about body and spirit and soul. As we'll see more than once, Jesus hesitates to heal the body and leave it at that. And as many of us know, sometimes he doesn't heal the body at all, but that doesn't mean he doesn't make us whole.

When the man rose and left, the crowd joined him in praise. This was a glorious moment. It included smiles and laughter. Surprise and awe. A little frustration on the part of the Pharisees, I'm sure, who lost some points here. I wonder if Jesus resumed teaching that evening. If so, the words had taken on new meaning in light of the healing they'd witnessed. Or did this open the door to more healings that night?

We'll never know, but we can assume the whole flavor of the gathering changed at that moment, and it never quite changed back.

Seen and Invited

The theme of this book is being seen and invited by Jesus, so we have to ask some questions. What did Jesus see that day? What was his invitation? What can we see here two thousand years out from the story with our cynical, tired eyes? What does this have to do with my broken road?

Jesus saw a man whose friends loved him. He saw a crowd that had no reason to believe he was anything more than a regular rabbi, a spiritual teacher. Israel had plenty of those. He saw a disciple who offered his house and ended up with a hole in his roof.

Jesus got closer, then, and saw a man whose spiritual needs surpassed his physical needs. He gathered that man in his spiritual arms and gave him the ultimate gift, forgiveness of his sins, knowing that was what the man needed for complete, eternal wholeness. He knew what those words would cost him, and he was more than willing to pay the price to complete this broken man.

What was his invitation? How was this man—and everyone in the room—changed by this encounter? The man, of course, walked away. Everything in his life changed. After this, perhaps he found a job. Perhaps he had a family. His relationship with the men who'd carried him surely changed, as now they would walk together and visit together in ways they never had before. Balance in those relationships was restored.

For everyone watching, Jesus invited them to understand his authority. Jesus the prophet wrapped his message in the actions of Jesus the shepherd. Likely that wasn't the only time Jesus healed that evening. Many were invited into the same situation. Jesus locked eyes with many broken souls. He took time with every one of them, and for a moment each one who found himself at Jesus's feet was given a smile, a word, a touch. For each and every soul, the story was different. Imagine the people of Capernaum comparing stories for days.

"He touched my hands when he healed them."
"He smiled at me. Did you see that dimple?"
"He called me son, even though I'm an old man."

Jesus came to Capernaum, staying in a fisherman's house, and touched many people. Each walked away with the invitation to trust this man, to see his authority, to taste the forgiveness of God given a human voice and a human touch.

Pulling it together

That's what can happen for you on the road of brokenness. Remember that it starts with proximity. You must make your way to Jesus's feet. You can walk or run or crawl. Maybe you need someone to lower you through a roof. But likely you'll find proximity through simpler means. Open the Bible and read the words. Pray. Worship with other believers. Whatever you do, stay close.

It's not a new thought. The Old Testament writers speak often of being near to God or in his presence. Try these on for size:

Surely you have granted him unending blessings and made him glad with the joy of your presence. Psalm 21:6

Better is one day in your courts than a thousand elsewhere; I would rather be a doorkeeper in the house of my God than dwell in the tents of the wicked. Psalm 84:10

The LORD is close to the brokenhearted and saves those who are crushed in spirit. Psalm 34:18

He tends his flock like a shepherd: He gathers the lambs in his arms and carries them close to his heart; he gently leads those that have young. Isaiah 40:11

The sentiment continues in the New Testament:

Come near to God and he will come near to you. James 4:8a

I pray that out of his glorious riches he may strengthen you with power through his Spirit in your inner being, so that Christ may dwell in your hearts through faith. Ephesians 3:16-17a

Proximity matters. Being close to God, close to Jesus, basking in his presence, dwelling in him… When Jesus was here on earth, people did crazy things to get close to him. We are asked to do no less. Get close. Cling. Dwell. Wholeness comes when we get close to Jesus, when we allow him to be our dwelling place, our fortress, the shepherd who leads us, the one to whom we bring our heartbreak and wounds.

If you're on the road of brokenness, start by sidling up to Jesus. Get as close as you can. He won't push you away. No, he'll look you in the eyes, crouch at your side, draw near, and gather you in. Along the way he'll see your needs—which aren't always what you expect—and invite you to live in new ways.

Unfortunately, being whole isn't always easy. Let's walk a little further down the road of brokenness and see a few consequences of being made whole.

Do You Want to Get Well?

Our next stop on the Road of Brokenness happens in John 5, where Jesus finds a lame man lying near a pool outside Jerusalem. The man is waiting for a miraculous stirring of the pool water, at which point he has a hope of being healed. John tells the story this way:

Afterward Jesus returned to Jerusalem for one of the Jewish holy days. ² Inside the city, near the Sheep Gate, was the pool of Bethesda, with five covered porches. ³ Crowds of sick people—blind, lame, or paralyzed—lay on the porches waiting for a certain movement of the water, ⁴ for an angel of the Lord came from time to time and stirred up the water. And the first person to step in after the water was stirred was healed of whatever disease he had. ⁵ One of the men lying there had been sick for thirty-eight years. ⁶ When Jesus saw him and knew he had been ill for a long time, he asked him, "Would you like to get well?"

⁷ "I can't, sir," the sick man said, "for I have no one to put me into the pool when the water bubbles up. Someone else always gets there ahead of me."

⁸ Jesus told him, "Stand up, pick up your mat, and walk!"

⁹ Instantly, the man was healed! He rolled up his sleeping mat and began walking! But this miracle happened on the Sabbath, ¹⁰ so the Jewish leaders objected. They said to the man who was cured, "You can't work on the Sabbath! The law doesn't allow you to carry that sleeping mat!"

¹¹ But he replied, "The man who healed me told me, 'Pick up your mat and walk.'"

¹² "Who said such a thing as that?" they demanded.

¹³ The man didn't know, for Jesus had disappeared into the crowd. ¹⁴ But afterward Jesus found him in the Temple and told him, "Now you are well; so stop sinning, or something even worse may happen to you." ¹⁵ Then the man went and told the Jewish leaders that it was Jesus who had healed him.
John 5:1–15 (NLT)

This might bring up questions. Did an angel actually stir the waters on occasion and heal the first person who stepped into the pool? Was Israel experiencing such spiritual outpourings at this time? Honestly, nobody can answer that. I have no problem with it. However, pagan religions of the time also had healing pools, which wouldn't be guarded by an angel to heal, so it's hard to say. Whatever the truth, this pool was surrounded by those hoping to find healing in the water.

Another question is what was Jesus doing there? A pool surrounded by the ill and broken wouldn't be a respectable location. The wealthy would avoid it. Those who worried about ritual cleanliness would avoid it, and that would include rabbis. Jesus, remember, had taken the role of rabbi, or spiritual teacher, which gave him the freedom to wander and teach and gather disciples. And yet, he surely made other rabbis cringe, because he didn't always follow the traditions rabbis would follow.

One of those traditions he broke as he walked among the broken and unclean that morning and stopped at the side of one particular man.

A strange question

When Jesus finds him, he asks the man, "Do you want to get well?"

This sounds like a dumb question. This man is sitting at a pool known for healing. Why would he not want to get well?

We don't really know why Jesus asked this question (It *wasn't* a dumb question!), but a common thought is that a miraculous healing for this man would change his life. A sick man made coins as a beggar. He likely had no skills. He'd suddenly change status. He'd have to work. Maybe his family needed his begging income. We don't know the specifics, but to a person used to life one way, making a change can be difficult. Jesus wanted the man to think through the consequences of being healed.

Honestly, I don't think of the consequences of healing in my life.

When I ask God for change, I don't think through what that change might mean. But Jesus knew. He understood what was about to unfold for this man who'd spent 38 years waiting for a miracle. And wow, the initial change wasn't what he expected.

The man wants to be healed, and Jesus tells him to stand, pick up his mat, and go, much like he told the man lowered through the roof. I think the command is significant. It's not about littering the world with mats. It's not about the uncleanness of a mat on which someone was sick or broken. It's the beginning of the invitation.

Remember, Jesus didn't simply see the broken in his midst. Being seen by Jesus is amazing. Having Jesus ask questions and interact and be interested in my life—I love that. I want to be seen and understood. I want to know Jesus understands all the implications of what he does for me, more than I know myself.

It isn't even about healing. We aren't healed for the sake of healing. We aren't healed and changed so we can lollygag around the world more complete than before. Sure, maybe we'd feel gratitude after that, but Jesus didn't heal people for their gratitude.

No, it's about the invitation. We are rescued and healed and put to work. It sounds a little mercenary, to be honest. Jesus spent his life putting together a work force. An army. He heals and sends us into battle. He puts a bucket of mortar in our hands and tells us to build a kingdom. As we dance around in joy at our new wholeness, he's dreaming up plans to put us to work. How is that fair?

An ancient purpose

Let's back up here. Way, way back. Back to a brand-new man, a brand-new woman, and a garden. One of the first things God tells Adam and Eve is to tend the garden. Genesis 2:15 says *The Lord God took the man and put him in the Garden of Eden to work it and take care of it.* He puts them to work. Work is part of our pre-sin lives. It existed in the world before sin broke the world. We are hardwired to be active. To be creative. To use our minds and bodies to benefit the greater community.

Sin changed that. After sin we try to get away without working, and I think that has to do with work being cursed. God said to work and multiply. Then we sinned, and he cursed those two areas specifically. Our deepest, most basic purposes are no longer good and life-giving and satisfying, so we run from them.

Jesus restores people on the roads and gives them a job to do. He puts us back to work, only he gives us the tools to do it. The curse isn't negated—how many Christians have terrible jobs or struggle with parenting? But in the spiritual realm, we work on a kingdom whose outcome is sure. When we walk the paths Jesus calls us to walk, we know the results. The kingdom WILL be built, and I WILL play a role. Failure isn't a viable outcome.

So what is Jesus's invitation to the sick man? It's simple. He tells him to stand, pick up his mat, and go.

I imagine the man's first, swift, gut response is to think *No, I can't pick up my mat. I'm a sick man.* Then half a moment later he smiles, because that's no longer true. Imagine the pride and joy on his face as he picks up that mat, something he hasn't done on his own for thirty-eight years, and goes. He goes where he wants. Mat in hand, proudly swinging it, so filled with joy he can barely see straight. Picking up a mat is simple to most of us, but if you hadn't done it in almost four decades, it would carry a world of significance. All doubts about his ability to do this, all his doubts about the man who'd healed him, disappeared as he bent without pain, lifted that mat into his hand, and left the pool area.

> More than once on our journey Jesus compares himself to water. In a desert land, fresh, moving, clean water is a treasure. Everyone knows of Jesus at the Samaritan well, and most of us know he compares himself to living water. But here Jesus stands at a pool of ritual cleansing and becomes the water. This man never dips in the pool, but he becomes clean. Jesus quietly takes the role of the pool in the man's life, cleansing him so he can engage in worship with the rest of his nation.

I wonder if he ever returned to that pool. I suspect not.

Stopped in his tracks

This is where the story gets a little darker. This is where Jesus's question gains significance. Jesus had a tendency to heal on the Sabbath. The Pharisees, in their zeal to bring God near with their spiritual fervor, had created a heap of rules around the Sabbath, completely losing sight of the purpose of the day.

Jesus, who uses every opportunity of his three years to teach and direct his people, spends a lot of time upsetting those Pharisees by reframing the Sabbath the way it was meant to be. That's Jesus living out his roles of prophet and king. This is one of those occasions.

The man gets caught carrying his mat. Yes, his life was just altered, he's wandering around in joy, and he is stopped for the crime of carrying a mat, a symbol of the huge changes he's experienced this day.[1]

I wonder if he simply blinked at them when they stopped him. Their charge must have seemed so petty to someone who'd just had his whole life turned upside down.

In the conversation that follows, the man admits he doesn't know Jesus's name. The man apparently had no idea a rabbi was walking around Jerusalem healing. I wonder if the Pharisees suspected who the man was talking about, if they were lurking and hoping to find more reasons to discredit Jesus, who didn't interact with the Law as they expected, who made them look foolish at every turn.

We can't know the answers to those questions. What we do know is that the man makes his way to the temple. He is clean and whole. Whatever illness had plagued him is gone. The next step for a good Jewish man would be to see a priest and be declared ready to resume regular worship again. Although we aren't told that's what this man was doing, it's a good bet he was seeing through the restoration Jesus had begun by healing him.

That's where Jesus finds him.

Think about that a second. *Jesus found him.* Jesus disappeared into the crowd without telling this man who he was. He gave him a simple invitation to pick up a mat. Walk wherever you want to go. Experience freedom you haven't experienced in thirty-eight years.

And he lets the man walk right into the hands of trouble. Then he shows up and finishes what he started.

Because wholeness isn't about a healed body. Like we saw with the paralyzed man, wholeness is all about the state of the soul, and this man needed one more thing before he was whole, before Jesus could consider this encounter complete and move on.

New perspectives

It was no coincidence the man was healed on the Sabbath and ran into trouble. All of that was part of the lesson. The world is hard and doesn't understand the truths of God, and this man experienced that. Was he afraid? Did he fear he would be put out of the temple, still unable to worship even though he was finally clean and whole? Or did he see the pettiness of the Pharisees compared to the power of the man who'd healed him and see these religious leaders in a new light?

Again, we can't know. But we know the man didn't give up on the temple, didn't give up on worshiping God, and that's where Jesus found him.

Jesus tells him two things: You are well. Stop sinning.

I don't think the warning to stop sinning had to do with an immediate sin. Jesus didn't catch the man mid-sin. It referred to the common belief that people were sick and lame and blind because of sin, and it was a warning for his future.

Jesus never indicates that the physically broken experience this because of sin. We'll see in two chapters that sometimes the opposite is true—He says a man is blind to reveal Jesus's glory. He says the same of Lazarus's death later in his ministry. However, Jesus uses the common belief to drive home a lesson. *Whatever the cause of your thirty-eight years of sickness*, he says, *if you don't turn from sin and toward me, this healing is useless, and those years will look like good years. Your future is bleaker than your past without repentance and faith in me.*

His body had been healed. Now Jesus wanted him to understand that a healed body isn't enough. Life isn't perfected because a body is healed. Life is perfected when a soul is healed, and the first step to that is repentance. It's what John the Baptist had said to hundreds.

It's what Jesus had continued to say. The message doesn't change. *Repent, for the kingdom of heaven is at hand.* Matthew 3:2 [John] and Matthew 4:17 [Jesus] (ESV)

The man had seen firsthand the power of that kingdom. He'd held a mat in his hand, a physical reminder of that kingdom. Now Jesus goes back to the repentance part. At this point, if the man heeds the warning, he is truly healed and truly whole.

It's so easy to accept blessings and not think about the changes they require. Am I willing to pay the price of wholeness? What mat might I be asked to pick up? Who is lurking in the shadows to cast doubt on my blessings, to scold me for my joy and obedience to a Jesus they don't understand?

Recently I encountered this personally. A few months before I began writing this book, I endured a bout of acute anxiety. I didn't feel well physically, had panic attacks multiple times a day, and barely left my house.

Then a doctor realized the panic was my body sending out a distress beacon. I was anemic, and it was getting worse, and I needed help.

Until then, for a few years I'd been struggling to accomplish things. I hadn't had many friendships. I spent most of my time on the internet alone, writing or publishing. I dropped out of church groups and friendships because I literally didn't have the energy to do it.

When my iron levels rose, I became a different person. I was able to stand again. I was able to pick up a mat. God hadn't left me while I was sick, but he hadn't asked as much because I honestly wasn't capable of as much.

But with healing came new opportunities. One was a request to write and read a devotional at a Good Friday service. My first inclination was to say no. Anxiety and illness was my excuse. I can write, sure, but standing up in front of people? Nope. Not what I can do.

Then Jesus waited, and like the man at the pool, I realized I was different. This was a mat I could pick up. Two months earlier it wouldn't have been possible, but I'd said yes to Jesus's healing, and now I had to live into my new abilities. My excuses had been stripped from me. I was more whole, and I was responsible for adding more bricks to the kingdom building project than I had done before.

I wrote and delivered a four-minute talk about Jesus's last words on the cross. People told me I did a good job, but that wasn't the point. The point was that I did it. What had been impossible was now possible. God asked more because I could do more.

The mats you can pick up will change as Jesus makes more and more of your life whole and well. So when Jesus asks if you want to be well, think about your answer. Are you willing to do more and be more and love more because you've been given more? Only you can answer that question.

Let's go back to the amazing moment when Jesus sought out this man to warn him about his future. The Shepherd doesn't heal us once and then walk away without a backward glance. When we need a warning or a course correction, or if we fall into yet another bramble, he seeks us out and helps us. The man wasn't left to face a hard world alone without the resources required to endure.

Because enduring is a huge part of wholeness. The endurance to stand and pick up a mat after four decades of being still. The endurance to face the senseless anger of others. The endurance to stop sinning because he'd been made well.

Perseverance

The responsibility of being made well is to persevere. Don't go on sinning, Jesus said. The horror of thirty-eight years of illness was nothing compared to the horror of returning to a life of sin without Jesus at the helm. The fear of being put out of the temple by the Pharisees was nothing compared to what would happen if God rejected him for his sinful, unchanged life.

The man had changed on the outside. Jesus then sought him out and made sure he had the tools to change on the inside.

Like I had the tools to stand in front of people and share. Was I nervous? Sure. But it was normal nerves and not the think-I'm-about-to-die nerves from my time of bad health. Jesus had to remind me that my old limitations were just that, old and outdated. I was new. And the man at the pool who could walk into the temple on his own—he was new, too.

One final note about our man from the pool. At the end of this passage, he finds the Jewish leaders who'd been looking for Jesus and tells them who healed him. Several commentaries said this was betrayal, that the man knew they weren't happy with Jesus, and he chose to side with the Jews against Jesus. Jesus healed him out of the blue. Then he sought him out to give him more information to complete that healing from the body to the heart level. The man's response? Betrayal.

Maybe. Other commentaries suggest this man was ignorant of the political and religious unrest swirling around him. If he considered Jesus and the Jewish leaders both to have some authority over him, he may have told the leaders about Jesus with no malice intended. I admit that, until I read the commentaries, I had never thought the man meant to harm Jesus. I prefer to think that he heard what Jesus said and changed his life.

Regardless, Jesus's actions show the shepherd again coming for the lost lamb. He entered an unclean place to find him, then reappeared to take his healing to another level. We can expect no less. Even the unclear end—Jesus approaches many of us, all of us, who don't deserve healing. Many in this world have food and water and shelter and health and yet never give thanks to God.

That's the kind of God we have. Our love for him doesn't dictate his care for us.

We've seen that proximity matters. We get close to Jesus and stay close. We've seen that healing isn't simple. A life of wholeness and wellness requires us to change how we see ourselves and how we respond to God. As we grow, he gives us more challenges, which cause us to cling harder to him and grow even more. Jesus wants his workers whole and thriving and well, and he comes for us when that isn't happening, just like the shepherd comes for the lamb trapped in the brambles.

From here, we'll head to one of the more amazing aspects of Jesus's healing, the power of his touch, especially when he applied it to the untouchable around him. Have you ever felt outcast and untouchable? Never fear, because Jesus waits with his hand outstretched to heal your brokenness and make you whole.

The Touch of the Shepherd's Hand

So far we've dug deeply into two stories along the road. Next we're going to look at a group of events linked by a common theme: Jesus's touch. Often Jesus touched those he healed, and many who came to him asked for this touch. What does it mean to have Jesus, son of the Living God, take time to touch you? And how can that apply today? I'd love for Jesus to look at me, smile at me, and touch me. So what does it mean that he did it then and can't do it now?

What makes these stories more amazing is that often those he touched were untouchable. Jewish people, following the tenets of God's own laws, didn't touch certain people. Some were unclean because of illness or injury or their situation. And yet Jesus found these people and touched them. He didn't touch everyone, but those he did... I suspect his followers cringed when he chose to touch some of these people.

Jesus doesn't differentiate. He held infants and touched lepers. Whether you desire a blessing, need a healing, or feel shamefully untouchable and hide from spiritual contact, Jesus wants to put his hand on you, the shepherd who both delights in the softness of the sheep and drags them out of danger and hiding to bring them home.

In a land where touch could bring about uncleanness, we are told over and over that those coming to Jesus asked him to touch them. Why? He shows more than once that touch isn't necessary for healing, so why is that what people asked for?

Here's my chance to dig into a little history. Biblically we see touch used in four different ways. Catch the sequence here, because it's fascinating.

First, touch was used to convey blessing—like Jacob touching Joseph's sons in Genesis 48 to bless them. Next, the laying on of hands was used to set something apart for God, be it a priest or even a sacrificial animal. Joshua was set apart this way by Moses in Numbers 27:18.

Third, Jesus and his followers used touch to heal. Then finally, the apostles laid hands on people to fill them with the Spirit (Acts 8:17). Think about this. Touch blesses us, sets us apart, heals and forgives us, and then fills us with the Spirit. Does any child of God *become* a child of God without each of these steps? We need each personal, specific, loving touch from God to become his sons and daughters.

The people of Jesus's day were most familiar with touch as a sign of blessing. Mothers called on Jesus specifically to bless their children with a touch, not asking for healing but for favor. Also, Greek healers often used the laying on of hands, so those in the Galilee area, especially, were familiar with touch and healing in tandem.

Even without the history or the Bible references, I think we intuitively know touch is personal, and we're seeing that Jesus deals with each of us personally.

So touch is both the people's and Jesus's method of choice for healing and dealing with people on the broken road.

Each one

Early in Jesus's ministry he is in Capernaum (before the paralytic and the roof incident), and we are told: *At sunset the people brought to Jesus all who had various kinds of sickness, and laying his hands on each one, he healed them.* Luke 4:40

It's pretty simple. And amazing. God came down as man and touched people. Lots of them. He personally blessed, set apart, and healed with the inherent power within his body. And, as I keep saying over and over because I can't get over how wonderful it is, he did it person by person, one at a time.

Now we step a little further down the road to two passages in Mark. In 7:32-36 Jesus heals a deaf man. In 8:22-26 it's a blind man. Between and surrounding these passages Jesus and his disciples discuss Jesus's identity.

Here's where we need to step back. Jesus is the Shepherd, here to tend the lambs. For younger me, he was a little girl's friend when she felt alone. But Jesus is also God. Priest. Prophet. King. He combines roles because he is, after all, one being. These two healings have multiple purposes and multiple lessons. We're going to hone in on one while not ignoring the others, because we can't tear Jesus into little pieces and fully know him.

First we have a deaf man. Like the paralytic, he is brought by friends. These friends ask Jesus to lay hands on him. Jesus then pulls the man aside, touches his ears and tongue (touches his tongue with spit, no less), and speaks. The man's ears are opened, and his tongue is loosened, and he speaks plainly.

By pulling the man aside, Jesus makes this moment private. Then Jesus communicates with the man what he intends to do by touching his ears and tongue. Perhaps this is the moment the man can leave if he doesn't want this, because we've seen Jesus give those he heals a choice. The man doesn't leave, and healing happens. Full, complete healing.

Now the blind man. We have some similarities to the deaf man. The man is brought by friends. Jesus is implored to touch the man. And Jesus leads the man to a private place. Also, again he spits on him.

We have a pattern here. However, this time healing isn't complete. The deaf man was healed in one shot. The blind man sees partially at first, and when Jesus touches him again, he sees clearly.

> What's with the spitting? Author Craig Keener suggests: *Spittle was sometimes associated with healing; it was also often considered disgusting and may have tested [the men's] desire to be healed.*[1]

Now the Prophet

This is where Jesus is showing us more than the Shepherd. Jesus is living out Old Testament prophecies, specifically Isaiah 35. The historian in me gets excited by these passages, because Jesus beautifully ties everything in history together. This passage reads like

35

this:

*Then will the eyes of the blind be opened
  and the ears of the deaf unstopped.
⁶ Then will the lame leap like a deer,
  and the mute tongue shout for joy.
Water will gush forth in the wilderness
  and streams in the desert.* Isaiah 35:5-6

The Israelites looked forward to this time when God would come to bless his redeemed. Jesus quite clearly indicates he has some role in this, which is another way of saying he is the One to come, the Messiah.

So Jesus isn't only a Shepherd. There's a bigger picture here. However, to keep from making this chapter book length, we're going to reduce our view back to these two men, because at the moment, they're not thinking big picture. They're glorying in their personal encounters with the wandering, healing rabbi.

What about the partial healing? It's the only time we see that, and I think a clue to why is again in Jesus's multiple roles. Between these two stories Jesus and his disciples speak about Jesus's identity, and it's clear they see partially, like this blind man. They're beginning to understand who Jesus is, but they're not there yet. They still don't have a perfect picture.

Just like the man. Jesus loves this man and heals him while also using him as an object lesson.

Okay, as we revel in the complexity of Jesus's three years here, we'll head back to the story.

Seen

In these encounters Jesus takes the men away from the crowds. Like Jesus narrowed his focus on the man at his feet in Peter's house, he narrows his focus by moving away from the chaos to deal with these two men. Disciples stuck around to witness this, because they were taking a three-year crash course in bringing Jesus's message to the world, but the public at large was absent. Both these healings are all about these two men and Jesus.

What does he see? He sees two men with friends who love them. He sees two men who struggle to live within society. He sees people who can't communicate the way the rest of us do, thus his need to touch the deaf man and bring the blind man to a quieter locale so he could be heard and understood.

He saw their weaknesses. He saw their relationships. He saw their futures, which weren't great in this society, and he changed them.

And the invitation? We'll get to that, but first let's back up in time a way and see this play out in a messier way with one more healing.

Untouchable

It's one thing to desire and ask for Jesus's healing touch in our lives, but it's another when that touch goes against everything society lives by. Our next visit is with a leper, a man considered unclean by the tenets of the Law, and a man Jesus, as a human rabbi, has no business touching.

The story appears in three gospels, and it's a great insight into how to approach Jesus and what to expect when we do. Mark tells the story this way:

[40] A man with leprosy came and knelt in front of Jesus, begging to be healed. "If you are willing, you can heal me and make me clean," he said. [41] Moved with compassion, Jesus reached out and touched him. "I am willing," he said. "Be healed!" [42] Instantly the leprosy disappeared, and the man was healed. [43] Then Jesus sent him on his way with a stern warning: [44] "Don't tell anyone about this. Instead, go to the priest and let him examine you. Take along the offering required in the law of Moses for those who have been healed of leprosy. This will be a public testimony that you have been cleansed."

[45] But the man went and spread the word, proclaiming to everyone what had happened. As a result, large crowds soon surrounded Jesus, and he couldn't publicly enter a town anywhere. He had to stay out in the secluded places, but people from everywhere kept coming to him. Mark 1:

40-45 NLT

First, a little background on this man's condition. Contracting leprosy changed a person's life. A leper had to live in isolation so not to spread the illness. It caused numbness, which resulted in easily damaged body parts. A person diagnosed with leprosy left his or her family and never lived in society again. Nobody healed from it. Some of the strongest Old Testament rules and rituals of uncleanness revolved around this condition.

This man, kneeling at Jesus's feet, had no hope outside of the healing rabbi. He comes with respect, humility, and submission. He asks for Jesus's willingness to heal, not demanding anything. He knows most rabbis would turn away from a leper. Even being close to one put a man at risk of being unclean.

Maybe the leper knew what he was asking, and he doubted a good outcome. Jesus had a reputation for healing by touch, and this man wasn't touchable. The whole of society agreed on that issue— *hands off this man. And just to be safe, ignore him and take the long way around to avoid him.* This man likely expected to be rebuffed, but again, Jesus was his last and only hope.

The bravery and faith that rested on its knees in front of Jesus was astronomical.

Jesus was moved by compassion. We're going to dig into Jesus's deep well of compassion on a later road, but I don't want to skip it entirely here. Jesus knew this man's fear, his bravery, and his dismal future. His heart allowed him to do nothing less than fix this situation.

This is where his followers cringed, because Jesus stretched out his hand and touched this man. Next to touching a dead body, it was about the most ritually filthy thing a person could do. But Jesus simply does it.

At that point, the man is clean. Skin healthy. He must have smiled. Maybe he closed his eyes when Jesus reached out his hand, unsure of what might happen, but now his eyes widened, and I'm sure he ran one clean hand over his other clean arm in wonder.

I read a lot about Jesus's state of cleanness at this point.

Ceremonially, he would now be unclean, but it would also have been clear to everyone around that this wasn't an ordinary situation. He is, of course, above the need to cleanse. He himself keeps proving to be the cleansing water, living water that runs clean from its source. Nobody he touched could ever affect his perfection and holiness. But we don't know if he went through the motions of the Law regarding cleanliness or not. The Bible never tells us that he does, but we also never hear the Pharisees complaining about him walking around unclean, so maybe he did cleanse according to the law, or maybe in light of the healing, it simply became a moot point.

But whatever happened ceremonially, Jesus was always clean, and his touch always cleansed.

Invited

Jesus had seen this man: his courage, his despair, his faith, and his hope. He'd reached out his hand and given the man the personal healing touch he needed. It was time for the invitation, and this one has a deeper meaning. It's time for Jesus to show himself as prophet again, to make yet another allusion to his full self as the Messiah.

He tells the man to go see the priest and make the sacrifices required for a cleansed leper. The cleansing for a leper wasn't easy. It required multiple washings and an animal sacrifice. However, it resulted in full restoration into Jewish society.

It also went a little deeper. This is one of those situations where Jesus has multiple lessons for multiple people. The last person healed from leprosy had been Naaman, 800 years ago, healed by the prophet Elisha (2 Kings 5). Lepers didn't get better. When this man showed up to the priest, the priest would have known someone different was in their midst. This healing would let Jesus link himself to one of the great prophets, Elisha, and move the priesthood a step closer to believing Jesus was who he was.

The man was also told to keep quiet, because crowds swarming Jesus for healing made it hard for him to get around. So he was told to endure the rituals of cleansing, informing the priests of the truth of the prophet in their midst, and to keep quiet so Jesus's ministry could continue unhindered.

It's unclear if he failed to see the priest, but he failed at the silence. The blind and deaf man would be given the same invitation to silence in the future, and they failed, too. The simple invitation to keep quiet proved too difficult, likely because they didn't understand what was at stake.

I wonder if I do that. If Jesus asks me to do something that makes no sense, do I balk? Do I make Jesus's job of reaching the world more difficult by acts of disobedience that seem small? I suspect I've failed Jesus similarly.

After this, Jesus had to move to remote areas. His work got a little more complicated, but it didn't slow him down. His compassion was as strong as ever. His hand was willing to reach out and touch the worst untouchables, such as Jairus's dead daughter in Mark 5.

You probably don't have leprosy. You might not be blind or deaf. And I'm pretty sure Jesus hasn't shown up at your church laying his hands on people to heal them. That being said, what makes these more than nice stories? They give credence to Jesus as God's son, but do they do more?

I sure think so. When Jesus draws those men aside to give them his full attention, I feel the calloused palm of the carpenter in my own hand, drawing me away from the chaos of life to find a place to spend time with me.

When a man on his knees asks Jesus if he's willing, and Jesus's heart swells with compassion, I know my humble requests fill Jesus with just as much compassion. My submission and respect matter to Jesus. Compassion spills over when I approach him as a child, as a lamb.

When Jesus has to touch a man's ears and lips to communicate his desire to help him, I know Jesus touches my own life, my own parts, my own weaknesses, that he's aware of my limits. He won't get frustrated when I don't understand. He'll find a way to reach me.

Even when I get ahead of Jesus and make my own way, ignoring his invitations and instead doing what seems right to me, I won't derail his plans or quench his compassion. He can forgive. He will forgive.

Now it's the Spirit who gets to hold my hand and touch my lips and spill cleansing water on my leprous soul. Better than Jesus in a way, the Spirit is with me always, Jesus's hands and lips and ears and feet always at my side and in my heart to heal my brokenness and invite me into the bigger story of kingdom building.

That touch is mine and yours. God uses touch to bless us, set us apart, heal our souls, and give us the Spirit, and once we have the Spirit, His touch is ours always.

True Wholeness

We're at our final stop on the brokenness road, the healing of a man blind from birth (John 1:1-41). At first blush it looks similar to the story of the man at the pool. They are similar in that Jesus heals, disappears, and then finds the healed men to further the conversation. Also, being healed leads both men into conflict with the religious leaders.

So I debated including this story, except it fills me with such joy. Jesus's compassion and the complexity of his nature are fully on display in this tale, and it's almost a blueprint of how to respond to a changed life, especially in the face of opposition.

Our passage is John 9:1-41. It's a long passage, so I'm only going to quote some of it here. Verses 1-7 go like this:

> *As he went along, he saw a man blind from birth. ² His disciples asked him, "Rabbi, who sinned, this man or his parents, that he was born blind?"*
> *³ "Neither this man nor his parents sinned," said Jesus, "but this happened so that the works of God might be displayed in him. ⁴ As long as it is day, we must do the works of him who sent me. Night is coming, when no one can work. ⁵ While I am in the world, I am the light of the world."*
> *⁶ After saying this, he spit on the ground, made some mud with the saliva, and put it on the man's eyes. ⁷ "Go," he told him, "wash in the Pool of Siloam" (this word means "Sent"). So the man went and washed, and came home seeing.* John 9:1-7

First, this is one of a few spots where Jesus explains the cause of suffering. Not that all suffering is for this reason, but in this case, this man is blind for the purpose of Jesus healing him and being glorified through that. Individual suffering often has a greater, glorious, eternal purpose.

But that doesn't make it easier to be blind or a leper or dead. God doesn't pass out painful circumstances to glorify himself and give no thought to the humans beneath the pain. No, Jesus is here to remedy this man's pain. He is the light of the world, he says, here to bring as much light as possible in his short time, and fixing brokenness was one huge way he lit the world around him.

The next part is fascinating. Jesus spits on the man (we recognize this from the last section—touch, spit, Jesus getting dirty and personal when fighting our brokenness), puts mud on his eyes, and tells him to go wash in a pool known, quite fittingly, as *Sent*. The man did so.

The man did so. Think about this. We are in Jerusalem on the Sabbath. This man doesn't know Jesus. Maybe he overheard the disciples talking about him. Maybe he'd heard of Jesus. But maybe a stranger put mud on his eyes and told him to wash, and he wasn't sure what to expect, but he did it anyway.

Later, he will tell the Pharisees that nobody is healed of blindness. And yet he trekked through Jerusalem to wash, so apparently a spark of hope and faith had already erupted in his heart at the rabbi's gentle touch and words.

The man doesn't go looking for Jesus. He goes home, and just like the man at the pool, his healing causes trouble. The man's neighbors are in awe, not even sure this is the same man, and they take him to the religious leaders, because it seems something outrageously miraculous has occurred.

A faith that grows

What follows is complex, so we're going to focus in on one aspect, the growth of this man's faith. As he spars with the leaders, he clings to a few powerful beliefs. Remember what Jesus said to the disciples at the beginning? Here it begins to be lived out. Through this man's suffering and cleansing, the work of God was displayed. Not just in healing, but in his attitude, his courage, his wisdom. The work of God didn't stop at the man's eyes. Light had entered his whole self, and that light would lead him to a dangerous, wonderful, amazing place.

The leaders interrogate the man, and through the discourse he says a few things he believes about Jesus. He starts out calling him *the man they call Jesus* (v 11) when speaking with his neighbors. When talking to the Pharisees, he calls him a prophet (17), a godly person (31), and claims he is from God (33). The harder the Pharisees push, the stronger this man's conviction that he was healed by someone special, someone God-sent and God-purposed.

This culminates after Jesus finds him, and the man ends by calling Jesus *Lord* and worshiping him.

The *man called Jesus* becomes a person worthy of worship. Why? Because God ordained to display his work through this man, to heal him, to light his understanding, and to pursue him.

We skipped over that part. Let's go back to it, because it might be the best part of the story. We're now in verses 35-38:

35 Jesus heard that they had thrown him out, and when he found him, he said, "Do you believe in the Son of Man?"
36 "Who is he, sir?" the man asked. "Tell me so that I may believe in him."
37 Jesus said, "You have now seen him; in fact, he is the one speaking with you."
38 Then the man said, "Lord, I believe," and he worshiped him. John 9:35-38

Jesus's healing had lit enough fire in the man that he defended Jesus to the Pharisees, not relenting even to the point of being thrown out of the temple. That's a solid conviction.

But Jesus knew this man needed more. He was now religiously adrift, and while he saw with new eyes, a few shadows needed removed. Like the man who only saw partially, our blind man only understands partially.

That's when Jesus shows up. I get goose bumps thinking of a cinematic enactment of this moment. The man is overjoyed at seeing, angry with the Pharisees, surely saddened at being thrown out. His parents didn't quite come through for him, and while we aren't sure of the motives of the neighbors, their actions didn't go so well for this man.

We need sad music and a close-up of a confused, dejected face.

Then the camera swings back. Let's start at a man's feet, sandaled feet moving with purpose. The music begins to swell. The camera pans up, up, and the music swells louder and more excited, until Jesus's face is in full view. This is the climax of our story. Jesus has come back to the rescue.

Except this man has no idea who he is. He looks right at him and doesn't know who he sees. Jesus uses that to his advantage and asks the man what he believes. The man expresses an interest in knowing more. He wants to know the man who healed him.

So Jesus tells him. Maybe the music needs to swell again here, because the man believes these words with ease, speaking his belief and following it up with worship.

This is the point when all the lights are on in this man, and brokenness gives way to wholeness. Yes, his body is healed. That happened early on. But it isn't until he confesses Jesus as Lord and worships that he is fully light and fully whole.

Seen and Invited

So let's go back to the sights and invitation here. What did Jesus see? He saw a divine appointment made before this man's birth. He saw a man whose parents had limited faith—they refused to get into the battle with the Pharisees as their son did—who begged near the temple. He saw a man with strong convictions and a sharp mind, able to hold his own against the Pharisees.

He saw a man who understood why Jesus had to be sent from God, who had more sense of God's character than the Pharisees, and a man willing to worship when God was clearly at work.

The disciples saw a man who was blind because of sin, and they could easily dismiss him. Jesus saw a future warrior, someone he would be proud to have building his kingdom. Jesus had set aside a bucket of mortar with this man's name on it from the beginning, and he was going to use it well.

What was the invitation?

It's simple. The invitations are often simple. Jesus wanted the answer to a question. *Do You Believe?*

One commentary had this to say about Jesus's question: *The question "Do you believe in the Son of Man?" is a summons to commitment, demanding a personal decision in the face of opposition or rejection.*[1]

The question was asked in light of what the man had just endured. *Are you willing to pay the price to believe? How deeply do you believe? If I reveal myself to you, what will you do?*

And the man's response—*Tell me more so I can believe fully.*

He wanted to know Jesus. While speaking with the Pharisees he'd worked out a few important ideas about Jesus and his closeness to God. Now he had the opportunity to understand more clearly, and he took it.

How deeply do I believe? Do I long for more and more knowledge about Jesus so I can believe more fully and worship him better?

Does opposition strengthen my convictions, as it did for this man, or does it weaken them?

And maybe the most important, do I trust that Jesus will come back? This man had no idea Jesus might seek him out. But I know it. I've seen it in the Gospels. And the Spirit is ever with me. Jesus will always come back. If I'm in trouble, in danger, in doubt, those sandaled feet turn around and come for me. That face is in my sights. Questions will be asked to guide me ever back on track.

Blind eyes and blind hearts

In the final verses of this passage Jesus dons his prophet persona and teaches a lesson. He says he has come into the world for judgment, to make the blind see and the seeing blind (v 39). Because of the next verses we can assume the ex-blind man is still with him. Maybe the man smiles, because this is almost an inside joke at this point. Both men know what the Pharisees said and did to this man in the name of knowledge and understanding. They understand how foolish the learned men appeared when sparring with a less-educated man.

But this moment isn't private. In fact, we find some Pharisees were with him, part of the crowd. These moments happened with an audience. This means Jesus sought out this man with crowds at his back. This wasn't something he did privately at the end of the day. No, the man wasn't finished displaying the works of God. This conversation, where the man confesses his faith and worships, happens with witnesses.

Again our man isn't hesitant in front of unknown people. He'll take on Pharisees. He'll confess something that just got him thrown out of the temple in front of strangers, and he will worship there in the road or outside the temple or whatever other location. Wherever it was, it was public.

The Pharisees take offense. They know Jesus is speaking of them directly, and his words hold a warning. *If you were blind, you would not be guilty of sin; but now that you claim you can see, your guilt remains.*(v. 41)

Now the man is an object lesson. He didn't claim to know who Jesus was. In fact, he only spoke of what he knew—his understanding of prophets, of God's dealings with sinners, and who holds the power to heal.

The Pharisees, on the other hand, simply insulted the man, called him a sinner, and cast him out. It's the debating equivalent of taking their toys and going home. They were losing the argument, so they became children.

So yes, their insistence that they weren't blind made them guilty. And this man who insisted on nothing except that a miracle happened and it had to involve a man from God—that man's eyes were opened. Jesus returned to him and gave him more information.

He had faith in what he understood, so Jesus gave him more knowledge so he could have more faith. The man who'd spent his life in the dark was given full access to the light. The men who thought they lived in the light discovered they were living among shadows.

These lessons aren't just for us. It's easy to look at the Gospels and see the Pharisees as the bad guys. But Jesus debated with them and showed them object lessons not just for us in the future, not just for the common man, but for the Pharisees themselves. The Jesus who sought out two men to make sure they were fully restored can also seek out the blind, the arrogant, the proud.

He held out hope to them. He explained things clearly. They had a choice given to them to trust what they saw and what they knew. Some, like Nicodemus, made the right choices. Blind men and seeing men can come from any place in society.

With healing comes an invitation to step into trouble. True wholeness leads us deep into a story that's been unfolding since the first moments. It also invites us into an ancient battle. We can count on danger. We know there will be opposition. The road is lined with shadows and will be to the end.

But we also know Jesus never leaves us. His sandals come our way when we need him. His Spirit never abandons us.

Proximity matters. Stay close to Jesus. His teaching and his love and his presence are vital to us becoming whole and useful and safe in his kingdom.

Accepting Jesus' healing means change, good and bad. We enter a big, colorful, exciting story, and those are never without drama and risk. But accepting those risks also means accepting big victories and big celebrations.

As we stick close to Jesus, we can expect his touch. He will bless us, set us apart, make us whole, and fill us with his Spirit. His calloused hand reaches for mine when I need it. His Spirit never leaves me.

And finally, true wholeness results in worship. When I am made whole by Jesus, I have no choice but to ask him to show me more and more of his beautiful self and to worship.

No, your brokenness isn't healed by reading one section of a book. But I hope this gets you excited. I hope you step into the next section feeling the hand of the Shepherd on your back, that you long for his voice, that you are excited to take more and more steps into the story.

From here, beginning to feel whole, we take on another road. Sometimes we doubt. We fear. We don't understand what God is doing, and trust is hard to find.

Don't worry. Jesus has answers for that. He dealt with many

doubters and fearful souls on the roads, and he'll deal with yours, too.

Section Two: The Dark Road of Doubt (and Fear!)

Doubt and fear. This road, filled with darkness, shadows, and ghosts, trips up many believers. Is God real? Is he true? Is he good? What if he doesn't come through for me…?

I find myself on this road more than I want to admit, so for me the stories here have special meaning. Maybe that's the case for you, too.

The most comforting thing to know about doubt is that God expects it. He doesn't want us blindly to believe things. He tells us to taste and see. Paul tells us to test the spirits. There are a lot of liars out there, false gods and idols trying to gain our trust, faith, and worship. It's okay to let Jesus convince you he is who he says, that God is who Jesus says. That's what the miracles were for. After centuries of silence, God was speaking to Israel in a big way when he sent Jesus, and they couldn't be expected to trust outright.

So ask God. Wrestle. Work out your faith and trust. And let Jesus help you as he gently, lovingly leads you off this dark, shadowed, haunted road toward the bright road of trust.

Sunk by Doubt

After Jesus fed the five thousand (which we'll look at later, because I've thrown chronology to the wind in this book), he sent his disciples ahead of him on a boat and retired to a mountain to pray. It had been a long day for both him and his disciples. Not only had he and his friends fed an enormous crowd, but Jesus had scattered that crowd and his disciples when it seemed the crowd might try to force him to become king.

The situation had gotten tense, and now Jesus recharged with his Father on a mountain.

Meanwhile, his disciples weren't finding as much peace. A storm came up, and they spent the entire night trying to cross the Sea of Galilee. Jesus saw this, waited, and then between three and six in the morning walked out on the water to save the day.

This is another beloved children's Sunday school story. Jesus walks on water. Then Peter, a character children can relate to because of his bombastic, loyal relationship with Jesus, walks with him. We have storms, miracles, heroics, an epic save... What's not to love in this story?

Let's give it a look, because this is a delightful story of doubt, fear, trust, being seen, and being invited. Children love it, commentators love it, and the more I read it and dug into it, the more I loved it. Jesus shows up in all his glory—the gentle shepherd, scolding prophet, authoritative king—combined so magnificently it's hard not to want to stand at his side and bask in his care forever. If ever a single story could draw people to Jesus, this is that story.

And it starts with fear, a whole lot of fear and frustration. Mark tells this part of the story this way:

Later that night, the boat was in the middle of the lake, and he was alone on land. ⁴⁸ He saw the disciples straining at the oars, because the wind was against them. Shortly before dawn he went out to them, walking on the lake. He was about to pass by them, ⁴⁹ but when they saw him walking on the lake, they thought he was a ghost. They cried out, ⁵⁰ because they all saw him and were terrified.

Immediately he spoke to them and said, "Take courage! It is I. Don't be afraid." Mark 6:47-50

Then we switch to Matthew, because he adds another dimension to the tale. John and Mark leave this part out, but this is where we're going to linger.

"Lord, if it's you," Peter replied, "tell me to come to you on the water." ²⁹ "Come," he said.

Then Peter got down out of the boat, walked on the water and came toward Jesus. ³⁰ But when he saw the wind, he was afraid and, beginning to sink, cried out, "Lord, save me!"

³¹ Immediately Jesus reached out his hand and caught him. "You of little faith," he said, "why did you doubt?"

³² And when they climbed into the boat, the wind died down. ³³ Then those who were in the boat worshiped him, saying, "Truly you are the Son of God." Matthew 14:28-33

Let's look at it a little deeper. First, Jesus dismissed the people from the meal and sent his disciples ahead. The disciples did as asked, possibly before dark, and they rowed between three and four miles. A storm came upon them, something that happens often on the Sea of Galilee, rolling down from the Golan Heights, so even these fishermen couldn't predict this and avoid it.

Also, their master had told them to go. Yes, Jesus sent them out into a coming storm.

When Jesus waits

It seems from all three tellings of this story that Jesus didn't rush to the rescue. He saw their plight from the mountain (probably miraculously in light of the storm and the hour), and instead of an immediate rescue, he waited. He sent them into the storm and let them sweat a little.

Why? We've answered that already, more than once. Jesus had lessons to teach. He had motives that made no sense to anyone but him and God. This was one of those lessons. Were the lessons more important than the people involved? Absolutely not. Once again Jesus beautifully weaves together his love for those in front of him and his love for those in the future who would read these stories. He alone can use three years of events to speak personally to thousands of people.

The men are tired. Exhausted. A long day followed by a long night. The joy of a miracle, the tension of the crowd, and miles of rowing. They had to be scared. They had to wish Jesus had come with them, because they had seen him still storms before (Mark 4:35-41). But they are alone.

Until they aren't. Instead, they see something that makes no sense. Someone is walking on the water toward them. It's dark and storming, and while they might expect Jesus to still the storm, they aren't expecting him to walk through it on the water. Would anyone expect that? Even with everything they'd seen, this was a little much.

So their first thought wasn't that Jesus had come to rescue them. Their first thought was ghosts or spirits, and their first reaction was fear.

Jesus's first reaction? To calm that fear.

The problem of fear

The tellings all agree that he calmed their fears immediately. He called out for them to take courage, told them who he was, and assured them they didn't need to fear.

Why would he wait around for the storm, but quell their fear immediately?

Because honestly, fear is more dangerous than storms. Fear gets us into all kinds of trouble. Mix fear and doubt together, and we find ourselves in hopeless messes.

Jesus wanted them to learn something about who he was, how he worked, and how he could care for them. He didn't want them afraid. Matthew Henry says it this way: *Christ will not be a terror to those to whom he manifests himself; when they come to understand him aright, the terror will be over.*[1]

Let that sink in. Jesus isn't out to scare you. And if you fear, likely you're not seeing things right.

I struggle with fear. Sometimes it's my fault, when I let my thoughts get away from me and dwell on things in the wrong way. Sometimes it's anxiety, which is more physical but can result in emotional fear. Jesus heals fear by letting me see him. The more I understand him, the less I fear.

Which is the lesson here. They needed to know who they were dealing with. And now they did. They might not have known the details of the virgin birth, that Jesus was literally, biologically the son of God, but they knew he was The One, the awaited one from God.

We're going to take a super-short detour here, because in the midst of this Jesus showed his ancient roots by living out Job 9:8: *He alone stretches out the heavens and treads on the waves of the sea.*

That one's for us. I guarantee the disciples at that moment made no connection between a few words in Job and what was happening in front of them. But for future people, or even for the disciples later on? Yep, Jesus takes every chance to assure us he is the long-awaited, ancient plan of God to save the world.

Seeing the disciples

Before we get to Peter and his walk on the water, let's deal with the disciples as a whole, because Jesus saw them and gave them an invitation there on the water.

What did he see? He saw exhausted men who trusted him and did as he asked. He saw their fear, knew their exhaustion could blow that all out of proportion, and quickly calmed that fear. The sea was scary enough; they didn't need to fear the rescuer. He saw their desperation. A storm is dangerous. These people needed a rescue.

Primarily, he saw his most beloved people in the world tired, scared, wet, and in need. His shepherd heart saw his lambs in trouble.

And his invitation? He invited them to peace. He invited them to trust his voice and listen to it as they'd listened to it hours ago. He invited them to let go of fear and cling instead to his words. Jesus's words cast out fear. Like his touch from the last section, his voice is just as powerful for directing us from the road of fear and doubt to the road of trust.

Proximity still matters

Now it's Peter's turn to get into the story. First, we can assume Jesus's words worked. If Peter had still been cowering in fear thinking a ghost was coming, he wouldn't have asked to come out on the water. No, he knew that voice was his master. He knew Jesus was here, so now the storm could calm, and things would be okay. He said "If...", but his actions show he's a whole lot more certain than an *if*.

Here's where the story gets fun, and it's open to some interpretation. Commentators don't agree on what happened here with Peter. Some say he was impetuous and had no business on the sea with Jesus, that he was showing off or acting out. I don't agree with those. I think the next part of this story is a beautiful picture of how Jesus had impacted these men and what they thought of him. And since they spent so much time with him, I'm going to trust their reactions.

First, Peter is Peter. We know he's pictured as hands-on, a man of deep loyalty who wants to be the best disciple he can be. He's the first to confess Jesus as the Messiah. He's the first to claim he'll die with Jesus.

It's no wonder he was the one out of the boat. But why? For one thing, he was a disciple. Disciples did what their masters did. Peter figured this was a lesson—as it was—so he wanted to try his hand at it. The Rabbi/disciple relationship wasn't all lessons in a circle at the side of the road. It was a relationship lived out. What Jesus did, they did. If Jesus walks on water, then I can walk on water.

Second, look how he asks. He doesn't leap out of the boat. He asks. And he doesn't ask to walk on water. He asks to come to Jesus.

Remember section one, the man coming through the roof?

Proximity matters. The disciples are tired, still afraid of the storm, and ready to be home, warm and dry. What's the best bet to see that happen? Get close to the master. Peter wanted to be where Jesus was. He didn't push. He didn't leap. He asked. *I want to trust, Lord. I want to know for sure you're going to rescue us. The wind and storm can't hurt you, but I'm over here in the boat, which is still tossing, and I'd rather be at your side.*

It's always safer at your side.

Those commentators who agreed Peter cried to Jesus out of faith and love and trust point out that Jesus didn't hesitate to call him. He didn't use this moment to teach Peter about humility or jumping out of the boat. He simply says *Come*.

It's pretty much how he reacted to the man on the roof. *Let them come. Those who seek me can come any way they want, and I will receive them.*

At this point Peter came to the end of his faith, but we're not going to blame him, because I'm pretty sure many of us wouldn't have stepped off that boat. We don't think to emulate Jesus that way. We don't always see the safety of proximity.

We doubt. We fear. And we let those doubts and fears determine how far we're willing to go with Jesus.

Sinking

Peter went into the water and successfully walked. We don't know how far he got, but he was close enough that Jesus could reach his hand. He did it. The man walked on water because he knew Jesus could make it happen.

Then he sank.

Why? He looked around. He realized what he was doing, where he was, and how crazy this all seemed. Walking on water in the dark in a storm? This was scary stuff.

I look around and sink, too. If I think too hard about events going on in the world or in my family or even in my own heart, down I go. Because I still think Jesus works within the system, and that means the system can overcome him.

But Jesus walked on the water. Nobody can walk on water. Did he float? Did he make the water hard? It doesn't matter, because it's impossible. Just like fixing the world or my family or my heart is impossible.

It's a good thing Jesus isn't bound by anything that binds me. What's impossible isn't impossible because he works things his way for the good of his people. Little things like the laws of physics can't stop him, so the workings of men in this world? Those don't slow him down, either. Because Jesus isn't bound by the way things are supposed to work, neither am I.

Peter was still bound. He wasn't sure of Jesus yet. He doubted that Jesus could do this, would do this. And down he went.

Then he says the first words that came to mind, and they were the perfect words. "Lord, save me."

That's all it takes. When I look around, when I doubt and fear, when I forget Jesus isn't bound by anything that binds the world, I only have to call out. There is only one save, and it doesn't matter if I call out while I'm on the top of the water, or when I'm to my knees, or if my head is underwater. I am a beloved lamb, and my call will be heard.

Jesus reaches out immediately. Again, this wasn't meant to hurt Peter. There is no penance to pay, no punishment for his lack. Peter had faith, and it wavered, and he called out to Jesus to save him. Jesus saved him.

It's that simple.

He saved him with touch. Peter could have floated. The water under him could have gotten hard. But you know what Jesus chose to do? He chose to insert his human body into the melee. He reached out his hand, and he touched Peter's skin. He gripped his hand, and he caught him.

Peter's relief at the touch of Jesus's hand must have been amazing. At that moment of contact, he knew all was well. The master had touched him. Hands that healed lepers and blessed babies now gripped him.

The storm had lost all its power, because Peter was now as close

The Dark Road of Doubt (and Fear!)

to Jesus as he could get. I suspect his full focus at that moment was the point of contact. He saw and felt nothing but Jesus's hand rescuing him.

As Jesus did this, he asked a question. Maybe the storm was already abating, because we assume Peter heard this question. Now that Jesus has Peter anchored, and the danger is over, it's time for a little scolding. He accuses Peter of not having enough faith, and he asks an important question: *Why did you doubt?*

This feels harsh. It's one of those things younger me always read and cringed. This is exasperated Jesus again. Except maybe it's not.

First, the disciples had seen a lot at this point. They'd seen five thousand people fed just the day before. They'd seen people healed. They'd seen Jesus stop a storm. How much would it take before they trusted Jesus fully?

Jesus showed here that he had the authority to walk on water. The authority to calm a storm. A man who can feed thousands with five loaves and walk on water is pretty much limitless. And yet… I think I will find that limit. Sure, Jesus came for me once. Sure, he can do anything. But will he?

Peter asked the same question. *Will he? What am I doing out here? Did Jesus really mean for me to be out here in the storm and not in the boat? What if he changes his mind?*

To an early believer, the question is about authority. Do God and Jesus really have the authority to do anything they want to do? But for those of us further along the path, the question becomes compassion. Will Jesus rescue me? Does he love me enough? Will he come through?

And Jesus showed Peter the answer to that when he grabbed hold of him. Yes, afterward he wanted Peter to understand that there was no reason to doubt, that his faith needed to grow in proportion with what he'd seen Jesus do. But first he rescued him. *Yes*, he was saying. *I will always come for you.*

Does that mean things work out like I hope? Nope. But am I forgotten? Am I left to drown in the storm? Will the world be allowed to sink me?

Also nope. Paul says it best in Romans 8: *For I am convinced that neither death nor life, neither angels nor demons, neither the present nor the future, nor any powers, neither height nor depth, nor anything else in all creation, will be able to separate us from the love of God that is in Christ Jesus our Lord.* Romans 8:38-39

Nothing stops Jesus from loving me. That means my soul is safe. My life is in his hands, first here on earth and later in heaven. He will not fail. His paths and plans may not be what I expect, but that love and rescue of my soul? That is a sure thing.

So why do I doubt? Jesus asked Peter that question. It's a question worth considering. Why do you doubt? Take the answers straight to Jesus and work through it. He comes in the storms. He pulls our souls through anything. We will finish the path and step into the rooms that await us.

Whatever makes you doubt, leave it in the sea and focus on Jesus. I'll try to do the same. But when we fail? His hand comes for us. Always.

We end the story with the disciples' reaction to this event. When Jesus and Peter returned to the boat, it's a little unclear what happened. The storm stopped for sure. They completed their journey across the sea. But maybe they rowed, or maybe Jesus moved them there directly, another miracle. (John 6:21 seems to indicate this one.)

Regardless of how they got there, they got there. But before they got there, they worshiped. They had the right reaction to what they'd seen. Jesus is worthy of worship. To Jews who believe only God is worthy of worship, this says a lot. They didn't see the *Job* correlation. They might not have understood the details. But they knew Jesus was the One sent from God, and he was worthy of worship. One final Matthew Henry quote: *They knew before that he was the Son of God, but now they know it better.*[2]

And that's the thing about doubt. Jesus simply keeps at us, proving his love and care, until we know it better and better and then let go of doubt completely and replace that with trust.

Seen and Invited

So, let's step back to Jesus looking at Peter. Peter was seen, understood, and given an invitation, and the result was a story that shows us the love and might of Jesus like no other.

What did Jesus see? He saw a beloved disciple who worked hard to be like Jesus, to learn from Jesus, to protect Jesus. We don't know much about the individual disciples, really, but this one was especially loyal and wanted to be close to Jesus in every way.

He saw a man who still carried doubts and fears, a man who didn't quite understand the big picture about Jesus yet, but a man who wanted to get there.

He saw a man who had the faith to get out of the boat but whose eyes would still stray. Did Peter surprise Jesus when he began to sink? Of course not.

Because Peter longed for Jesus's relationship and love and teaching, he got to be part of some of the best lessons. Scary and humiliating sometimes, but also long-lasting and legacy-forming.

How about the invitation?

It was simple. Jesus said *Come.*

That's it. If you're in a storm, or in a boat, or anywhere, doing anything, and you ask Jesus if you can get closer to him, his answer will be the same. *Come.*

But once you start to follow, don't look around. Don't think about the systems around you and how far outside of them you might be walking. Simply come. If you think you don't have the faith? That's fixable. His hand will catch you, and in time you'll walk it with less stumbling. The command was to come, and if he asks you to do it, he'll make sure you can comply.

Come. Have you heard that lately and not followed? Maybe today is the day to brave the storm.

And along the way, between the gusts, make sure to worship.

One final thought before we move on, and I have to add this because I still love the Psalms of David. Warren Wiersbe makes this connection in his commentary on the Old Testament.[3] That day and the day before, the disciples had lived out Psalm 23. Jesus had led them, and five thousand others with them, to green pastures, feeding them their fill. Then he had taken the disciples from the storm to the port, leading them to still waters.

The result? The continued, further restoration of their souls. Doubts were lessened, trust was grown, and the authority and compassion of Jesus was better understood. Some of the final words of this Psalm became more real in their minds: *Surely your goodness and love will follow me…*

Jesus came for them. He followed them. He quelled their fear, honored their faith, and taught them that they had a way to go. He comes for you, too. He comes for me. In the storms he is capable of a rescue, and his heart for you requires a rescue. When you doubt and sink, call out and stretch out your hand. You will not be disappointed.

From here we move to a small, simple story that might be the prayer I pray the most. Read on as Jesus continues to lead us from the roads of doubt and fear to the road of trust.

I Do Believe

The next stop on the road of doubt and fear takes us to one of the most honest prayers of the Bible, one I have prayed many times. Since God knows me so well, why not be honest?

We focused on fear more than doubt with Peter and the disciples on the sea, but this story is heavy on doubt. (No surprise, we're going to combine the two quite well in the third one.)

Our passage is Mark 9:14-29, and it reads like this:

14 When they came to the other disciples, they saw a large crowd around them and the teachers of the law arguing with them. 15 As soon as all the people saw Jesus, they were overwhelmed with wonder and ran to greet him.

16 "What are you arguing with them about?" he asked.

17 A man in the crowd answered, "Teacher, I brought you my son, who is possessed by a spirit that has robbed him of speech. 18 Whenever it seizes him, it throws him to the ground. He foams at the mouth, gnashes his teeth and becomes rigid. I asked your disciples to drive out the spirit, but they could not."

19 "You unbelieving generation," Jesus replied, "how long shall I stay with you? How long shall I put up with you? Bring the boy to me."

20 So they brought him. When the spirit saw Jesus, it immediately threw the boy into a convulsion. He fell to the ground and rolled around, foaming at the mouth.

21 Jesus asked the boy's father, "How long has he been like this?"

"From childhood," he answered. 22 "It has often thrown him into fire or water to kill him. But if you can do anything, take pity on us and help us."

23 "'If you can'?" said Jesus. "Everything is possible for one who believes."

24 Immediately the boy's father exclaimed, "I do believe; help me overcome my unbelief!"

²⁵ When Jesus saw that a crowd was running to the scene, he rebuked the impure spirit. "You deaf and mute spirit," he said, "I command you, come out of him and never enter him again."

²⁶ The spirit shrieked, convulsed him violently and came out. The boy looked so much like a corpse that many said, "He's dead." ²⁷ But Jesus took him by the hand and lifted him to his feet, and he stood up.

²⁸ After Jesus had gone indoors, his disciples asked him privately, "Why couldn't we drive it out?"

²⁹ He replied, "This kind can come out only by prayer." Mark 9:14-29

This is another story told in three gospels, but Mark spends more time with it than any other writer. Before we dig in, though, we need to know what comes before, because it's important. Jesus is once again living out OT events and speaking clearly of his role as King and Messiah, and that will play into our story.

Jesus, John, James, and Peter had been on a mountain, probably Mount Hermon, where Jesus transfigured. The disciples saw his glory, and Elijah and Moses came to speak with Jesus. On the way down, they discussed John the Baptist being the Elijah promised in the Old Testament.

As this story unfolds, Jesus has about four months left on the earth. This is crunch time. He's about to go, and final lessons are being learned. The disciples have come far, having been given authority to do miracles and preach and then successfully doing these things.

One of the final lessons happens on that mountain. The trio that witnessed it is told to be silent until after the resurrection. They don't understand, but they do obey.

So what did they learn, and what does it have to do with an honest prayer that some of us continue to pray so far into the future?

Old Testament echoes

When Jesus heads up that mountain, he's showing them the future. And he's fulfilling the past. In Exodus 24 and 32, Moses goes up and then comes down the mountain to get the Law. Moses takes Joshua; Jesus takes his inner three. A cloud covers Moses and Joshua as a cloud covers Jesus. The voice of God speaks through the cloud in both stories.

Then Moses comes down the mountain to find his brother has been talked into making an idol, and Israel is worshiping it. Their faith had waned during Moses's absence, and they filled that space with something familiar to them, idols like their Egyptian masters.

This takes us to our current story, where Jesus comes down the mountain and finds a mess, too. The disciples tried to exorcise a demon while he was away, and they'd failed. Crowds had gathered, because where the disciples were, the crowds assumed Jesus would be. And the religious leaders were here to argue with the disciples, likely mocking them for their failure.

It is not going well at the bottom of the mountain. It's not quite a gold calf and a dance to false gods, but considering the final exam for disciple school comes in four months, this is not a good scene.

Jesus asks what's happening, and we get our first glimpse of the man at the center of the story, the man who will cast an interesting light on the rest of the players. The man tells Jesus this whole mess has to do with his demon-possessed son and the disciples' inability to cast the demon out.

Here we get exasperated Jesus, and I'm not making any excuses for him. This isn't day one or two of these men's discipleship. The crowds have seen three years of miracles. The leaders have debated Jesus a thousand times.

And yet, nothing seems to change.

What Jesus says to the disciples—and maybe to the leaders and the crowds as well—tells us just how static things truly are. Mark says Jesus calls them an *unbelieving generation*. Matthew adds *perverse and unbelieving generation*.

Let's pop back in time. Remember how Jesus just reenacted Moses's climb up the mountain to get the law? Some say that was a coronation of sorts for Moses. Well, Jesus just did the same. The final leg of his journey is starting, when his job as Messiah culminates, and soon he will be gone.

In Deuteronomy 32 God has Moses write a warning to Israel, because they will become corrupt not long after Moses is gone. Verses

5 and 20b read like this: *They are corrupt and not his children; to their shame they are a warped and crooked generation. ... for they are a perverse generation, children who are unfaithful.*

Moses loved Israel. He got between them and God's anger more than once. He called out on their behalf. And yet they exasperated him.

Jesus is echoing this call. He's about to sacrifice everything for them, and they are breaking his heart. As they squabble like they always have, like their ancestors always had, he walks alone toward his final moments, and he knows many of them will walk away. Many will be killed. His sacrifice won't instantly bring about a kingdom of light and glory.

So yes, Jesus is exasperated. A day ago he basked in God's glory and reflected that glory to his closest friends. Today it's back to the grind.

David Garland quotes it this way: *Jesus expresses in a complaint "the loneliness and the anguish of the one authentic believer in a world which expresses only unbelief."*[1]

An honest father

Jesus finishes this anguished cry by asking for the boy to come to him. The father, of course, is listening to this, and now we're going to focus in on this man who hoped to see his son whole.

First, his son has been like this for a long time. He tells Jesus that the spirit hurls his son into fire and water. The boy foams at the mouth, and his teeth gnash. I assume this poor father—and probably mother— hasn't been able to leave his son unsupervised for five seconds in years. Then he discovers the whereabouts of Jesus, who witnesses say can expel demons, and he arrives filled with hope.

That hope isn't long lived. Jesus is missing, and the disciples who try to help him fail. The religious leaders pounce, and a debate and argument ensue.

Whatever faith this man had took some good hits that afternoon. Maybe this demon is too strong. Maybe his story won't have a happy outcome. He wasn't counting on failure and anger and arguing.

But now the rabbi is back. Hope unfurls, but it's not as strong as it was. This has gotten messy, and he's doubting everyone involved.

Jesus asks him how long his son has been like this. In the middle of it all, Jesus focuses in on this man and his son. The demon, not happy with what's about to happen, puts on quite a show, but Jesus focuses not on the boy nor the demon. His focus is the father.

He sees the father. He questions him. He takes time to deal with this situation, leaving his disciples and the squabbling leaders for another time. This is the father's moment.

If you can do anything for us, take pity on us and help us.

That's the father's reply. It's polite. It's uncertain, but so far the rabbi's entourage has not impressed. The man is honestly admitting that right now, he's not sure what to expect.

Jesus gets right to the heart of the matter—doubt and fear and faith. This demon story has very little to do with a demon. This is all about the dad. The man says, *If you can, then help.* Jesus turns it right around—*If you believe, I can help.*

No, the disciples haven't impressed. No, the arguing among the leaders and the disciples is worrisome. But Jesus takes those characters straight out of the story.

It's you and me, Jesus says. *You and God. What do you think I can do for you? Because that's what I can do for you.*

If you believe

This can be horribly misunderstood and misused. Jesus isn't saying a person with enough faith can treat God like a wish granter. And we know sometimes we pray with faith and God has other plans. We can look back and realize God's plans were better plans. So when he says *Everything is possible for one who believes*, what does he mean? This is important, so we should make sure we understand.

I went overboard on the commentaries for this one, because I honestly wasn't sure. And I think we'll let John answer this question, which boils down to heart motive, love, and obedience. Here's what Jesus says to his disciples in John 14 when they are discussing Jesus leaving and them finding him and seeing the Father:

I Do Believe

> *¹² Very truly I tell you, whoever believes in me will do the works I have been doing, and they will do even greater things than these, because I am going to the Father. ¹³ And I will do whatever you ask in my name, so that the Father may be glorified in the Son. ¹⁴ You may ask me for anything in my name, and I will do it.¹⁵ If you love me, keep my commands.* John 14:12-14

If we love him, keep his commands, seek to glorify him, and hope to do the works Jesus did, then we can ask in his name and expect Jesus to do what we ask. There are a lot of conditions there, but it boils down to proximity again. The closer we are to Jesus, the more we will reflect him and ask things that will build the kingdom. Jesus always gets behind building the kingdom.

Casting a demon out of a little boy definitely counts as something Jesus would do, and if this man believes that, his son will be healed.

Oh, the pressure. The man's honest assessment of himself leads us to the prayer that has come down through the ages. *I do believe. Help me overcome my unbelief.*

How does Jesus respond to this? Exactly like he did to Peter's heartfelt cry for rescue in the sea. He acted. After being exasperated by the unbelief around him, he challenges this man to believe, and when the man admits he harbors doubt, Jesus doesn't scold him. He doesn't lecture or roll his eyes.

He simply fixes the situation. Because this is faith. I suspect not one of us has full, complete, never-doubting faith. Yes, the disciples should have known more, again because of their experience with Jesus. This man didn't have that. All he had was poor faith, doubt, and desperation.

In his commentary on *Mark*, author Steve Wilmhurst suggests the man's thoughts are something like this: *'Yes, I believe you can do something; but I have nothing else to offer. I'm pleading with you to help, because I have nowhere else to turn and no other resources.' We have a word for that. We call it: praying. The man is doing what the disciples did not do. He is praying; and Jesus answers his prayer.*[2]

I can come to Jesus in doubt. I can admit my faith is weak. When

Peter sank, Jesus reached out an arm, and that same thing happens here. No matter how exasperated Jesus is with me or with my generation or with anything around me, he longs for me to ask for stronger faith, and he is willing to come whenever I honestly call.

Jesus heals this boy. The demon leaves violently, and the boy appears dead, but Jesus takes his hand—that mighty skin contact again—and helps him to his feet. The word Mark uses in the Greek denotes resurrection. The boy appeared dead. Even in life, he was barely living. Jesus restores him and hands him back to his father.

We don't know how the man or his son react to this. We only know this boy won't be facing demons again. We know his father's faith is stronger now than when he set off this morning, and he understands his role in seeing his prayers answered.

Instead, we end with the disciples. Jesus was exasperated with them, but he doesn't turn away. He doesn't give up. Instead, when they ask what went wrong, how they failed, he tells them. It's time for a little private debriefing.

In *Mark* Jesus simply says it's a matter of prayer. In *Matthew* he expands on that and says it's because they have so little faith. They have been given the authority to do things in Jesus's name, not on their own power, and it seems here they had gotten a little arrogant and forgotten the source. They have to be close to God, not just at the moment of healing, but all the time.

Like the man came to the end of himself when calling on Jesus, they needed to come to the end of themselves, too.

Have you experienced spiritual victories that led to a fall because you began to think it was about you? I struggle to read book reviews for my books because sometimes they include praise, and I can start to think I'm hot stuff. Look at my talent. See how well I put words together?

But as a child of God, my victories have to do with being connected to the vine, with my closeness to Jesus, with my surrender to the Spirit.

The tension between knowing I'm doing things well and remembering who enables me to do things well—that tension needs to remain intact and not tip to the side of me thinking I'm the source.

The father demonstrated the right way to approach Jesus, admitting we need him and we can always trust more and honor him more and glorify him more.

The original title of this chapter was *Jesus is Glorified by my Unbelief*. I think that's still valid. The disciples' belief failed. The man's belief wavered. But Jesus stepped off the mountain into the fray and displayed his glory. I can't derail Jesus by my faith or lack thereof. He is central to all things.

Seen and Invited

Let's step back to the middle of the story and look at the players again, seeing if we can glean what Jesus saw here and determine the invitations.

The spiritual leaders, you notice, were completely ignored. Jesus didn't seem to speak to them. His actions were about to speak louder than any words, and he wasted no words on them.

The disciples had failed. They didn't know why, since they had done this before. They had the authority to cast out demons, but their faith in Jesus wasn't strong enough. That means their faith had to be somewhere else. Nobody tries to cast out demons without confidence in something.

So Jesus saw his disciples making the same mistakes as the ancient Israelites at the bottom of the mountain, thinking they could arrange their spiritual victories on their own. There might not have been a golden calf involved, but they were looking elsewhere when they needed eyes and hearts fixed solidly on Jesus and His Father.

He saw a boy with no life, no hope, a vessel for evil who never had a chance, a boy with parents who loved him and cared for him and would do anything for him. He saw a boy worthy of a future, a boy who could one day hold a job and have a family and live a normal life if evil would release him.

And he saw a desperate father trying to decide what was true and real. Were the disciples truly doing God's will? Why had they failed? Were the spiritual leaders right, and these men had no power?

The Dark Road of Doubt (and Fear!)

Where was the rabbi, and if he showed up, could he do anything?

He saw a man honest from the beginning, asking politely for help after his hopes had been dashed upon the disciples' failure, a man whose repentant cry for help and faith resulted in the healing of his son.

And the invitations. He invited the disciples to pray, to get right with God, to remember they weren't healing on their own but using God's power. They had no idea how vital these lessons were or how little time they had left to learn them.

He invited the man to trust, to give up doubt and believe. *If you're going to ask me for help, then you need to believe I can give it.*

Jesus spent time in this passage exasperated, but that didn't curb his love. It didn't make him turn from his lambs in need. His heart was open, and his hands were active. My fears of dealing with exasperated Jesus come to nothing, because he's not a mere human who gets angry and spites me or makes me pay penance. Just like Moses told God not to send the Israelites to the new land if God's presence wasn't with them (Ex. 33:15), Jesus won't deny us his presence if we are behaving badly.

I feared that Jesus would get exasperated with me because I'm a worrier, a doubter. I don't doubt Jesus's power, but sometimes I doubt his heart, his love. I'm not alone in that, so stories like this are included in the Gospels where people just like me, who are still working out their faith, can come and find victory. People just like me, who sink in the waves or stand on the edges not sure of the players, or, like our next story, hope to love Jesus without attracting his attention—He meets all of us here on these pages. In three years he knew all his people and made sure each of us would find ourselves, our fears, and our weaknesses on the roads of Judea.

Steve Wilmhurst summed up this story beautifully: *Into the middle of this turbulent crowd of characters comes Jesus the Messiah; he takes control, applies his authority and banishes the evil. This is the message: you need to have faith in him.*[3]

Have faith in him. It can start small. It almost has to start small. But keep applying it and let Jesus grow it bigger. Know where that faith and the victories come from, that it's not you, and know that even when you fail, Jesus is still the Shepherd, and you are still the lamb.

Why do you doubt? I asked it at the end of the last chapter, and I'll ask it again, because the answer means something. Why do you doubt? What do you doubt? Is it God's existence? His power? His heart? Some of all of them? He longs to talk to you about whatever it is. Chances are someone in the Bible doubted in the same way, so get close to the Scriptures and find those souls. God is the same now as then, so his answers for those doubters is the answer for your doubts, too.

Just remember Jesus responds to your honest desire to trust more deeply. He wants to show you his glory and use it to help you fulfill his plans for your life.

Our final stop on this road of doubt is a well-known tale about a woman whose faith is praised by Jesus, but when we look at it, it's a hesitant faith at best. So let's see what Jesus can do with a morsel of faith and how that can heal a life and a soul and even play a role in raising the dead.

An Incomplete Faith

We saw Peter's faith fail. We saw a father admit he never had that much faith to start with. Now we find a pair whose faith is strong but incomplete, allowing doubt and fear to fester.

Jesus loves our faith, even when it's small, broken, or incomplete. And our final story shows us yet again that he longs to demonstrate to us that he alone is worthy of our complete trust.

This is another well-known tale usually focusing on Jesus's treatment of women. And it is definitely a beautiful story about how much Jesus values women, but we're going to touch on that and move on, because whole books have been written on that subject already, and because I don't think his focus was this woman's sex. His focus was much, much deeper.

However, the context has everything to do with her status in society as a woman, so we'll start there.

In college I took a course on women's history taught by a non-Christian. She pointed out that ancient Israel stood out from the nations around it in its treatment of women. The dowry system was flipped from most others in that a father didn't have to pay a groom to take his daughter. Instead, he was paid by the groom. A houseful of Jewish daughters was a financial boon. In certain cases, a woman could inherit land. Women could become judges (Deborah) or prophetesses (Miriam).

Unfortunately, by the time Jesus arrives on the scene, things had changed. The Jewish views had been affected by Greek and Roman influences, so women were not valued as they had been. A second century BC Jerusalem scholar Ben Sirach wrote many things speaking against women as dangerous and only having value in relation to men, and these ideas permeated Jesus's times.[1]

This is the situation at our next stop on the road of doubt and fear. A ritually unclean woman sees in Jesus her only hope of healing and rescue, but she has to get through society's defenses to get there, so she hatches a plan, a plan Jesus both admires, compliments, and then destroys.

Meanwhile, her story is inextricably connected to that of a synagogue leader, and Jesus will weave his moments with them together, loving them and then teaching both them, the disciples, and the crowds even more about doubt, fear, and Jesus's desire to earn our trust and faith.

So, let's head a few more steps down this road and experience one final story before we jump roads again.

Two characters

Told in three gospels, the story of the bleeding woman is half of a full story that includes a man named Jairus. We see Jairus first, a synagogue leader and therefore a devout Jew who asks Jesus to heal his daughter. (Note how he values his daughter. This is important.) Jesus agrees, and they head toward Jairus's home. Mark tells it like this:

When Jesus had again crossed over by boat to the other side of the lake, a large crowd gathered around him while he was by the lake. ²² Then one of the synagogue leaders, named Jairus, came, and when he saw Jesus, he fell at his feet. ²³ He pleaded earnestly with him, "My little daughter is dying. Please come and put your hands on her so that she will be healed and live." ²⁴ So Jesus went with him. Mark 5:21-24

For Jairus all is well. The healing rabbi is at his side, about to save the day. He breathes easier, maybe for the first time in days. Peace and life are about to be restored to his world.

Then the whole thing falls apart, because the rabbi stops, looks around, and begins asking who has touched him. In a throng of people, it's an odd concern. And frankly, Jairus has bigger concerns. Time is ticking out for his daughter, and Jesus is worrying about a single touch in a throng that bumps against him constantly.

Now we step away from Jairus toward the other player in our story. Mark continues like this:

And a woman was there who had been subject to bleeding for twelve years. ²⁶ She had suffered a great deal under the care of many doctors and had spent all she had, yet instead of getting better she grew worse. ²⁷ When she heard about Jesus, she came up behind him in the crowd and touched his cloak, ²⁸ because she thought, "If I just touch his clothes, I will be healed." ²⁹ Immediately her bleeding stopped and she felt in her body that she was freed from her suffering. Mark 5:25-29

A woman had joined the crowd who suffered from a condition that had rendered her unhealthy and ritually unclean for twelve years. The assumption is this is some type of menstrual bleeding that wouldn't relent. (The former anemic in me feels her fatigue). Because of this, she couldn't have marital relations, so she probably wasn't married. She had spent all her resources on doctors to no avail. This woman, like most of those we meet on the road, has no hope outside of Jesus.

However, as an unclean woman, she doubts she will be welcomed into Jesus's presence. She isn't a synagogue leader like Jairus. She isn't bold like the blind man or the leper. Her fear of rejection forces her to come up with Plan B. She will sneak up on Jesus, syphon off a little power, and be healed.

She planned to tap into Jesus's power without tapping into Jesus's person. She trusted the prophet's strength, but she doubted the Shepherd's heart.

Being unwelcome

Does this resonate at all? This was my decades-long fear, too. I didn't want to meet exasperated Jesus and find myself unwelcome. I thought I might sneak into the kingdom without quite attracting the attention of the Son along the way.

In pagan religions of the day, with their petty, all-too-human gods, many rituals were meant to turn the eyes of a god away.

Humans were safer when gods ignored them, so humans followed rituals to the letter hoping the gods would barely see them.

This woman was working on the same premise. She felt safer sneaking under Jesus's radar.

She touches him, and it works. She feels renewal in her body. I wonder if the healing was so complete that her iron levels were normal, the color returned to her cheeks, and she felt a spring in her step she hadn't felt since she was a girl. It had worked. The power of God had come through the prophet to heal her.

Jesus stops, and I imagine he smiles. Maybe he hid the smile, because this next part was going to be fun, but he had to take this woman's fears seriously. This brave, frightened woman was about to be seen in the deepest way, and she was about to discover her physical healing was only the first step in a deeper healing. Her doubts, fears, and isolation were about to give way to a new kind of life.

Let's let Mark tell us the next bit:

30 At once Jesus realized that power had gone out from him. He turned around in the crowd and asked, "Who touched my clothes?"
31 "You see the people crowding against you," his disciples answered, "and yet you can ask, 'Who touched me?'"
32 But Jesus kept looking around to see who had done it. 33 Then the woman, knowing what had happened to her, came and fell at his feet and, trembling with fear, told him the whole truth. 34 He said to her, "Daughter, your faith has healed you. Go in peace and be freed from your suffering."
Mark 5:30-34

Jesus wouldn't let her leave without dealing with her heart. She had to meet not only the Prophet but the Shepherd. She hadn't been healed yet, not completely, and part of that had to do with her doubts about his heart and her fears concerning her welcome.

She falls at his feet in fear. So again, she becomes the center of his frame of vision. She and he share the closest thing to a private moment that can happen in this crowd. Luke tells it this way: *In the presence of all the people, she told why she had touched him and how she had been instantly healed.* Luke 8:47b

What does Jesus say to this? Matthew tells us he starts with *Take heart.* Some translate it as *Take courage. Don't be afraid.* Something wonderful had happened to her, and her powerful faith in God's power had done it. He didn't want her trembling in fear after such a victory.

He follows up by calling her *daughter.* That's the welcome. Daughters are always welcome. She needed to know that hiding had been unnecessary. Even as an unclean female, her faith assured her welcome. Jesus found her valuable regardless of her condition or situation or the culture in which she lived. From here out she would know that Jesus the rabbi had welcomed her. He had seen her on her knees after she'd broken highest protocols and touched his clothes while she was unclean, and he had spoken to her with love and welcome.

Next he compliments her faith. Her faith had been incomplete and hesitant, but it was enough. He's about to help that faith along by introducing her to the Shepherd. Now she can know Jesus the person as well as Jesus the prophet, and she can trust both. Doubts are stilled as Jesus looks down at her with compassion.

Finally he blesses her. He sends her on her way in peace. She has twelve years to make up for. She might go find a husband. She might have a child. That starts now, so he sends her out to live the changed life he's just given her.

The word for peace is transliterated *eirene,* and it has a component of reconciliation, of peace between parties. Peace between her and God, her and Jesus, her and her religious community. It also speaks of welcome. Her fear of being welcome is put fully to rest by Jesus's actions and his words.

Although she's at his feet, and he is focused on her, the crowd witnesses this. I think the reason he made her tell her story was to restore her to her community. In fact, I almost included this story in the fourth section about Jesus restoring community, but I thought her doubts were more important. However, Jesus makes her do this in a public setting so everyone around would know she was clean.

Yes, he says to the crowd. *I introduce to you my daughter, whom I love, who is no threat to your cleanness and can now participate fully in your world.*

The woman learned the power of her own faith, the power of Jesus the prophet, and the power of the love of Jesus the man. Then she leaves with a blessing of peace and restoration.

Waiting in the wings

Meanwhile, Jairus is still with us. I imagine this man is crawling out of his skin with impatience. He was so close. The rabbi had been on his way. He'd felt such hope, and now Jesus stops for this whole other drama. Finally, after what must seem like an eternity, the scene with the woman draws to a close.

That's when the servants arrive and inform him it's too late.

His world stops. What did he experience in that moment? Shock? Disbelief? Anger? Grief? All of the above?

Jesus jumps in right away. He doesn't give Jairus time to lose hope. Remember the sea, when the disciples feared? Jesus stopped their fear as fast as possible. He does the same for Jairus's doubt, because I feel safe saying Jairus at that moment doubted Jesus could help him. That window had closed the moment his daughter drew her final breath.

Jesus tells the man not to fear but to believe. Mark simply tells us Jesus said to believe, but Luke tells us he told the man to believe and his daughter would be healed.

I wonder if Jairus did believe when Jesus told him to. Honestly, in the depths of his heart, did he think Jesus would heal his dead daughter? We'll never know for sure, but he does take Jesus home with him.

People point out that Jesus calls the healed woman *daughter*, something he calls nobody else. He also tells her that her faith has healed her. The word he uses in Greek is related to the word for believe he uses with Jairus. So in the span of a couple minutes, Jairus sees Jesus heal a daughter because of belief, and then Jesus immediately uses this same idea for his own daughter. I wonder if that simple repetition of words calmed the man, or if, at this moment, there is no calm to be found.

They get to Jairus's house, and the room is cleared of all but the girl's parents and Peter, James, and John. Jesus takes her hand, speaks to her, and helps her to her feet. She is alive.

He then tells everyone in the room to stay quiet, and he feeds this girl, much like he himself will eat after his own resurrection, because there's nothing quite so human and vital as eating.

The bleeding woman is healed in public. Jesus doesn't tell anyone to stay quiet about that, and we later see other times when people touch Jesus's clothes for healing, so maybe that started here. People saw what had happened and shared the story.

But healing the dead is something else. The people aren't ready for this one yet. But he brings in witnesses, because the time will come when the story needs to be told.

Seen and Invited

Whew. I admit I typed all this out fast. It's an exciting story. But now that we've looked at the facts, let's slow down and back up and see what these two travelers experienced on this road and what it means to you and me on our roads.

Let's start with Jairus. What did Jesus see when he faced Jairus? The man is a synagogue leader. He has servants. He is a man of standing. He loves his daughter. We learn she is twelve, so she's nearing marriage age, and she's about to lose her whole future. Jairus has enough faith in Jesus's ability to ask him to come to his home and lay his hands on his daughter. Jesus stretches that belief to the edge and maybe beyond, but Jesus sees that the man has enough faith in God and in Jesus as God's follower to expect a miracle here.

Jesus invites Jairus to take him home. Then he invites Jairus to believe, to trust, to entrust himself to Jesus. Luke says Jesus explicitly tells him healing will follow, but that might be implied. Whatever the case, the man was asked to trust the unthinkable, that this man Jesus had the power not only to heal but to restore life. That's a big jump, but Jesus asks it.

And it's couched in simple terms. *Believe. Trust. Let go of the doubt. Rely on me for the next step, which is simply walking to your house.*

We're called to the same thing. The end game isn't always spelled out, but the call is simply to entrust ourselves in Jesus and walk the next step. Take Jesus home. Let him in. See what he'll do with your grief and hope and pain and doubt.

Regardless of what Jairus expected, he took those steps and walked the rest of the way home with Jesus.

The second invitation is one we've heard before. *Keep quiet.* This is a strange invitation. It was in the earlier cases, and it is now. Sometimes what Jesus does for me is to be shared with the masses, and sometimes it's just for me. God's timing is his alone.

Jesus helps out in this case. I find it amusing that Jesus sowed a little doubt along the way. He tells the mourners the girl is asleep and not dead. They laugh, certain she's dead, but when the girl reappears alive, they will doubt. The rabbi said she was asleep, and now she's alive, so maybe…

The story got out. We don't know who told it, but those faced with the wonders of Jesus seem to struggle with silence.

Now back to our bleeding woman. Oh, Jesus had so much to see here. Desperation. Cleverness. A strangely shy boldness. A little sly underhandedness. Fear. Faith. Faith based on partial understanding, but no less faithful.

And he saw more, things she may not have realized. Her need for reconciliation with her people. Her need for peace and security based not on her physical condition but her heart.

The invitation? Again, we have two. The first is to come into the light. He creates quite a scene getting her into the open. This time it's the disciples' turn to be exasperated, because they had no idea how to find one person in a crowd crushing against him.

But he doesn't relent until she comes forward, fearful and trembling. After living a shadow life for twelve years, her moment in the light has come, and he means to get her out there where everyone can see. He seems to admire her plan as the faithful gesture it was, but it wasn't enough. She has to tell her story and entrust herself to

Jesus the same way Jairus will. Jairus did it by taking Jesus home. The woman does it by stepping into the scene.

Because the theme of this story is trust. Doubt and fear become faith and trust. This is about reconciliation with God, with families, with the community, and it starts with trust.

His second invitation is a blessing. *Go*, he says. *Go in peace*. Start a life without suffering. Do things you couldn't do before. Participate and blend in with everyone else, because you're one of them again.

Sometimes the invitation isn't to do something wild and amazing. We aren't all called to lives like Paul or Peter or John. Sometimes the call is to belong, to live our lives in front of everyday people doing everyday things while showing them that even that is a blessing from God.

Personally, I don't always appreciate the simple blessings from God until I lose and regain them. Maybe I can learn to thank God and appreciate the daily blessings without suffering loss.

Doubt and fear darken a life. They give the enemy cover to take our thoughts. Jesus tells his people many times not to fear, but he also demonstrates it in stories like these, proving himself worthy of trust.

We saw Jesus reach out his hand to Peter in his doubt, not in anger but in love. He longs to rescue us from the dark places when doubt sinks us.

We saw that Jesus, even exasperated, wants to see our faith grow. I don't have to hide my doubts and fears. Instead, I can admit to him my failings and expect him to honor and bless my honesty.

Then finally, we saw that incomplete faith is all Jesus needs. He simply asks us to take the next step with him. Join him in the light and take him home. As we do, our faith grows. He calls us sons and daughters and welcomes us wherever we are on the path to complete trust.

We're heading off to a new road after this. We've seen Jesus restore wholeness to broken people. We've seen him dig down into our doubts and fears and show himself patiently worthy of our trust. Now he steps onto the road of discontent and restlessness, that winding road where we chase anything that moves in our quest for fulfillment.

And he will show us that he is it. Fulfillment comes from Jesus alone. And he can prove it.

Section Three: The Twisting Road of Discontentment

Discontentment. Restlessness. Yearning. The never-ending quest for something new, something exciting, something to fill the empty spaces. This road is barely a road. It's a maze with a whole lot of dead ends, and many of us get trapped in this maze and never escape, whiling away our hours and days trapped in little nooks and crannies and never moving again.

I've heard people say they don't want to trust God because of the limits. They hear the *Do Nots* of the ten commandments and think loving Jesus means denying ourselves life's pleasures and experiences, that life with Jesus is limited and small. Many of us fear that in Jesus our needs won't be met, and we will lose what most matters to us.

On the roads we'll encounter in this next section, Jesus throws out this idea by showing that he alone can give satisfaction. Only through Jesus do we find fulfillment—in our relationships, in our physical needs, even in our mental need to understand. Yes, Jesus cares about your curious soul. Whatever you think you'll give up by following Jesus, he restores that beyond your imagination, because God made us and knows exactly how we work, what we need to grow and thrive, and what fulfills us.

The idea that God wishes us satisfied is seen many times in the Old Testament. He gives us everything we need, but he goes further and speaks of satisfied souls.

Moses asks God to *Satisfy us in the morning with your unfailing love, that we may sing for joy and be glad all our days.* Ps. 90:14

David says of God that *The eyes of all look to you, and you give them food at the proper time. You open your hand and satisfy the desires of every living thing.* Ps. 145:15-16

God himself speaks to Jeremiah in a dream assuring him that, after the captivity of Israel *I will refresh the weary and satisfy the faint.* Jer. 31:25

God makes us whole. He asks us to trust him and not fear. Because he is the author and creator of everything we have and everything we are, he is also the only one who can truly provide what we need for a satisfied, fulfilled life. And it seems he wants this for us. He loves us and wants the best for us.

The melancholy writer of Ecclesiastes sums it up well: *That each of them may eat, drink, and find satisfaction in all their toil—this is the gift of God.* (Ecc. 3:13) God satisfies us as a gift because he loves us.

That's where we walk next, off the road of discontentment and need and onto the path of true fulfillment and satisfaction.

In Need of a Drink

We begin our journey toward the road of fulfillment at a well. John 4 tells us Jesus was in Judea, but he needed to leave because the authorities were unhappy with him, so he headed home to Galilee.

Most Jews would make this journey by going toward the Jordan River and around, avoiding Samaria. Jesus, however, heads straight through Samaria, because it seems someone—or several someones—needed a gentle nudge from a wrong road to the right one, and it starts on a road that leads to an ancient well on a hot afternoon.

Because this story is long, and because so much has been written on it, we're going to pick and choose where to settle and what to look at. This chapter is about Jesus fulfilling needs. He didn't simply heal wounds. He didn't only treat those afflicted with doubt and frozen by fear. Jesus cares about our fulfillment. Our discontented, restless souls mean everything to him, because he knows the key to true fulfillment. And he shows us this when he sits on a stone well and waits for a woman who knows one of the most difficult modes of this restlessness: broken relationships.

Nothing makes us more discontent and restless than wanting intimacy and finding only brokenness, and the woman walking toward this well knew a lot about broken relationships.

Let's set the stage with John 4:

⁴ Now he had to go through Samaria. ⁵ So he came to a town in Samaria called Sychar, near the plot of ground Jacob had given to his son Joseph. ⁶ Jacob's well was there, and Jesus, tired as he was from the journey, sat down by the well. It was about noon.
⁷ When a Samaritan woman came to draw water, Jesus said to her, "Will you give me a drink?" ⁸ (His disciples had gone into the town to buy food.)

⁹ The Samaritan woman said to him, "You are a Jew and I am a Samaritan woman. How can you ask me for a drink?" (For Jews do not associate with Samaritans.)

¹⁰ Jesus answered her, "If you knew the gift of God and who it is that asks you for a drink, you would have asked him and he would have given you living water." John 4:4-10

Time to visit my inner historian. A few facts clarify what's going on here, and they're important to see what Jesus did, why he did it, and what it means for those of us wandering a road of discontentment.

First, he's tired. Don't you love that? Jesus, God in man, has the human weakness of fatigue. He didn't pretend to be tired to meet this woman. He was tired. Walking Judea from one end to another, healing, speaking, and teaching take it out of a person. Jesus needed to rest.

Second, he was thirsty. Again, there's no reason to think this isn't real. He's sitting at the well, worn out from eluding the Pharisees and leaving Jerusalem, sitting on a stone well cap exposed to the sun in the heat of the day, and he needs a drink.

So, when a Samaritan woman approaches, he asks for her help.

This throws her, and to fully understand her reaction we need a little history lesson. The Samaritans and Jews didn't get along. And that's the kindest way to say that. They hated one another. The Samaritans worshiped on Mount Gerizim, within sight of this well, and Jews had destroyed their temple on that mountain almost two hundred years earlier. Samaritans had sneaked into Jerusalem and vandalized their temple. They didn't trust one another, didn't interact, and certainly didn't ask one another for water.

Jesus asked anyway.

An unusual encounter

Let's back up to the woman before she responds to this unusual request. Imagine her on her way to the well. She's doing a few odd things here, and those things might tell us about her thoughts on this afternoon. First, she seems to be alone. Women traveled to the wells together to collect water in the mornings or evenings, and they traveled together for safety and companionship.

So our Samaritan woman is out here alone in the heat of the day. She has nobody to help her with her jar, as the women would help one another lift the heavy water-filled jugs onto their heads or into straps to make them easier to carry. Something about this woman isn't right.

To make it worse, she approaches the well and finds a man sitting on it. She's now alone with a strange man at the well in the heat of the day. Then she gets a little closer and realizes he's a Jewish man. Like it couldn't get worse. She knows men, but Jewish men... This man will hate her. He might mock her. Perhaps he'll assault her. Her miserably hot and lonely task just got worse.

How did she know he was Jewish? It might have been his clothing—as a rabbi he would wear a tunic with tassels and perhaps a phylactery, things seen on many devout Jewish men. Or perhaps she didn't know until he opened his mouth and a Jewish dialect or accent spewed forth. But whatever gave him away, our woman is wary.

Then Jesus does the unthinkable. He asks her for help.

I love this, too. He's tired, thirsty, and vulnerable, sitting at a well with no bucket. Likely his group carried a small rolled-up leather bucket, but it had gone ahead with the others. Jesus is at this woman's mercy to have his thirst quenched. His need is real, and he earnestly asks her to help him.

Daniel T. Niles says this of Jesus's request: *"The only way to build love between two people or two groups of people is to be so related to each other as to stand in needs of each other."*[1] To draw this woman close, he has to expose himself as human. He's about to make her vulnerable, and he begins by making himself vulnerable.

Her answer gives away some unease. She's rude and flippant, perhaps out of fear, perhaps anger. Jews aren't kind to Samaritans, so this might be a trick. The man looks weary, but he still might hurt her. If nothing else, he could mock and belittle her for her heritage. She just wants to get her water and return to the shade of her house.

But something in his answer... Living water. He's at a well talking about living water, the water that runs through rivers and creeks and springs, fresh, cool water that's easy to get into a bucket. She's about to spend time lowering and lifting buckets of water seventy-five feet down a well to fill her jar, and the thought of a nearby spring she didn't know about... She has to know more.

Jesus is more than willing to accommodate. This woman is as weary as he is, and he knows that. He knows all about her. He sat himself in this very spot on this very warm day to meet her and talk with her and ultimately rescue her.

They discuss water a little more, because she is thinking this man has literal water that will keep her from ever having to haul water in the heat by herself again. And he, of course, is speaking of himself and the Spirit that will come after him, a life of quenched thirsts and fulfilled hopes and adventure and purpose. Not a life spent hauling water day after day that doesn't fill her soul.

I have no husband

Finally, even though she doesn't understand yet, she asks for this water, and Jesus changes the conversation. He digs right into the heart of the matter, her deepest thirst. He asks her to bring her husband.

She responds that she has no husband, which is true, but it's hiding something. Jesus knows what she hides, and he pushes forward. John tells it this way:

> *"I have no husband," she replied.*
> *Jesus said to her, "You are right when you say you have no husband. [18] The fact is, you have had five husbands, and the man you now have is not your husband. What you have just said is quite true."* John 4:17-18

And there it is, a possible answer to why this woman is hauling water alone in the heat of the day. Also, we get a deep look into a discontented, restless, disappointed soul. The Samaritans had similar views on marriage and divorce and adultery as the Jews, and because of her past she didn't measure up or fit in.

For those of you who are married, think back to your wedding day. Remember hope, joy, new love? Remember how exciting it was? The Samaritans kept many of the same laws and values as the Jews, so this woman was expected to marry young and then stay married. Her community would have celebrated this with her.

But it all went wrong. We don't know the details. Was she divorced? Widowed? Abandoned? All of the above? Had she been excited on her first wedding day, possibly a teenager about to step into a new life, a new status in her community? What had happened? How had she dealt with it?

Then she found herself married again. Was it her idea? Was her father behind it? Was she as excited this time? Was she wary? Were her hopes a little dimmer this time?

Then she went through this a third time. A fourth. A fifth. Were her later weddings celebrations, or did they happen in private? Did she hope at all of finding intimacy? Were there children, or did that hope die with the end of each marriage? Did her family get excited for her? Did they show up? Did family even acknowledge her by her fifth marriage?

All five failures could have been someone else's fault. Or they could have been her fault. But whatever happened, this woman was not familiar with emotionally fulfilling, thirst-quenching marital relationships. She had disappointment after disappointment behind her. And because of that, she might not have had female friendships, either, because she didn't fit cultural norms.

Then her current situation would be the most damning. At this point she's not married, but she has a man. Does she love him? Is he married? Does she need him to support her? The fact that she tells Jesus so lightly that she isn't married could be taken as flirting, so perhaps she's tired of number six and looking for number seven.

When Jesus exposes her relationship failures and sin, she breezes right past it. Many commentators say she's humiliated and wants to avoid that topic. They might be exactly right. But beyond that, to me she simply seems disillusioned and tired. Whatever hope and joy that young bride had six men ago, it's gone now. She'd rather discuss the finer points of religion with a strange Jewish man than her failures.

Wouldn't we all? I admit I do the same thing. Sometimes I study the Bible as a scholar while avoiding Jesus in prayer. Just the facts, thank you. I'd rather not dwell on my weaknesses or sins or failures. Let me sit at Jesus's feet and listen to him speak instead of fielding his questions as he and the Spirit dig into my soul to unearth sin and tend wounds.

Questions for the prophet

Jesus lets her change the subject. He doesn't condemn her with his words; he simply states them, and she decides he's a prophet.

At this she seems to perk up. She has a few things to discuss with a Jewish prophet, questions about worship. Because for all her disappointing marital life, she seems drawn to the idea of worship. Even if it's a cover for her true feelings or a way to get Jesus to back off the personal, her topics are real, things she's considered. At least it seems that way, because Jesus takes everything she says seriously.

Think about that. She's a Samaritan woman, one who's engaged in at least some form of sexual sin, and Jesus takes her seriously.

Kenneth Bailey says this of the whole conversation, and I think he sums it up beautifully: *Jesus accepts, cares for, takes seriously, challenges, recruits and inspires a simple Samaritan woman with a life-changing message centered in himself.*[2]

The fact that she sticks around to converse with Jesus after he points out her sinful lifestyle says she didn't feel threatened. She felt accepted, at least enough to keep talking. Jesus was tired and thirsty, and even though she considers him a prophet, he's also human. She no longer considers him a Jew out to humiliate and mock her. She's gotten comfortable with the man and the conversation.

It's here where Jesus first corrects her. He doesn't say anything about her marriages, but he assures her that the Jews are right and the Samaritans wrong about worship and God. But he tempers that by pointing out that soon it won't matter. Something is about to happen that will make the long-standing feud of worship in Jerusalem vs. worship on Mount Gerizim obsolete.

That change is him. Jesus is about to take away the main point of contention between these two people groups. Both the Jews and the Samaritans will flounder when Jesus dies, returns, and establishes a new covenant.

But that's secondary to the heart of this conversation. This conversation isn't Jesus's attempt to change the religious beliefs of the Samaritans through one unmarried, adulterous woman.

No, the point and the heart of the conversation is, from beginning to end, the soul of this one unmarried, adulterous woman. That was the point when Jesus let his disciples go ahead. It was the point when he settled on a hot rock in the heat of the day. It was his point at every twist in this conversation.

I want to take an aside here. In a minute the disciples will return and find Jesus talking to this woman at the well. They trust Jesus enough not to give him grief about it, but John mentions their surprise. Once again, Jesus is doing what isn't supposed to be done.

Also, their Jewish training is real, and they can't help but think about a few men in their history who had interactions with women at wells, namely Jacob, Moses, and Isaac's servant. The result of those interactions? All three men ended up married to someone met at a well.

So, do you think they wondered if Jesus was thinking similar thoughts? Rabbis could marry. But would Jesus ever marry a Samaritan?

Well, they might have been with him long enough to wonder. He touches lepers and spits on the eyes of blind men. He's not the most predictable rabbi.

Or maybe these thoughts never passed through their minds, but I suspect in hindsight it passed through John's as he wrote these words down.

An unlikely proposal

That day the Samaritan woman, after years of unsatisfying, unfulfilling, disappointing, heart-hardening relations, sat at the well and was drawn in a by a lover who wanted to quench her deepest thirsts. What Jesus offered—the spring of eternal water, the worship in spirit and truth, and the prophetic understanding of her deepest hurts—was a betrothal.

She had the opportunity to know intimacy in a way she never had before. She had the opportunity to be a Samaritan who knew the depths of God's love and truth. She had a chance to discover answers to her deepest questions about both God and herself.

She could be loved. What Jesus offered was no less romantic than a young man standing at her door promising her fulfillment and contentment and love if she became his wife. This was a spiritual marriage proposal to a woman who had had her share of marriage proposals, all of which had disappointed her.

Her response? She doesn't jump at this. Instead, she says the Messiah will make it clear. She exposes a longing in her people that also lingered in her own soul. Answers. One day she'll have the answers, because God had promised to send someone to make sense of this broken, discouraging world where she resides, where she walks alone without friends to get water every day in the heat, water that never entirely quenches her thirst. She isn't convinced this Jewish man has those answers, even if he's a prophet, but she trusts they exist and can solve her problems. Jesus smiles. I know John doesn't say that. I'm adding this on my own, but I am sure he smiles before his response. Sometimes he uses these words with force, invoking their full authority, but this woman didn't need that. She needed something more tender. She needed a smile, the gentle nod of a head, and the reassurance that her longings could be fulfilled.

She says the Messiah will bring her the answers she seeks. And Jesus gets to tell her, using the phrasing of the Old Testament, who he is. Here's how the TLV version, a Bible translation presented by the Messianic Jewish Family Society, puts it: *Yeshua tells her, "I—the One speaking to you—I am."* John 4:26 (TLV)

I am. The Samaritans knew their Pentateuch. She knew those words for what they were. This man who knew all about her might have her answers.

Before we move on, let's dig into a couple places to make sure we see the big picture.

This woman didn't approach Jesus. She didn't sneak up and touch his cloak. She didn't join a crowd. She had no idea who Jesus was, and even when she had a vague idea, a Jewish rabbi with prophetic tendencies didn't do much for her.

> The Samaritan idea of Messiah comes from Deut. 18:18, where God promises to send another prophet like Moses. They weren't expecting a military savior like the Jews. Instead, their Messiah would be a teacher helping them understand how to live for God. To the Samaritan woman, Jesus easily filled this definition.

So this one is all Jesus. I love that. A few people I love aren't impressed with Jesus, either. They're not seeking him. But that doesn't matter. Jesus can seek. He can ask the right questions, dig down into the right dark places, and bring a person's hopes, fears, and dreams to light.

I know a few cynical Samaritans, and they're no match for a tired rabbi sitting on a well. I take comfort there.

Come and see... and change

The disciples return, and the woman leaves. She leaves so quickly that she abandons her water jar. She plans to return, because she's about to take Jesus up on his first invitation, or a least a variant of it. She's going back to her village to bring others to hear.

Get your husband and come back, Jesus told her. She does one better and brings back many. What makes this amazing is that they came. I wonder how her village felt about her. It always surprises me that they listened to her. She draws water alone. Maybe the women are afraid to leave her alone with their husbands. Maybe the men like her too much, or maybe they ostracize her.

But that day she'd been invited to draw up living water. She'd been invited to give up the religious question of where to worship and to see worship and God in a new way. A prophet who treated her well, maybe better than anyone treated her, had piqued her interest and her curiosity. Maybe long-dormant hope had been roused, both in her personal life and in her spiritual concerns.

And the village saw it. Whatever they thought of her, when she appeared without her jar and excitedly told them what she'd experienced, they needed to see for themselves. Apparently this longing for a Messiah was as strong in them as in the Jews, and they didn't want to miss the opportunity to know the truth.

While they're gone, Jesus speaks with his disciples about food and priorities. Just as the woman took his water metaphor literally, they take his food metaphor literally. And while it's a fascinating, worthwhile conversation, we're going to table it, because the woman and the village are on their way back. Jesus spoke to the disciples about a ripe harvest, and they're about to see it.

The Samaritans ask Jesus and his disciples to stay for two days. Again, this isn't normal. There was a saying among the Jews that eating any Samaritan food was the equivalent of eating pork flesh, something they were forbidden to do. Accepting their hospitality? No.

But they do. Jesus shows them a Jewish man who knows them, who can fulfill their religious curiosity and straighten out their misunderstandings. He reads their hearts. Through him they see their relationships with one another and with God in a new light.

It's a very exciting two days.

Things changed in that village. I wonder if the woman's status changed. I suspect it did, that her human relationships became more fulfilling as her relationship with God changed. I wonder what happened in the village a few years down the line when news of Jesus's death and resurrection reached them.

A few commentators mention Acts 8, where the deacon Philip flees to Samaria when Christians in Jerusalem are under attack. He casts out demons and heals, and so many Samaritans welcome him that Peter and John are sent from Jerusalem to lay hands on them so they can receive the Holy Spirit.

I wonder if any from the town of Sychar were in that number, if the whispers from this town of an encounter with the Messiah primed the pump, preparing people to believe. I wonder if they laughed at the realization that this was the fulfillment of Jesus's mention of no longer worshiping in either temple. Maybe this woman was there, and she described this conversation to John and Peter, a private conversation at a well that ends up in this gospel.

Seen and Invited

Regardless, Jesus sought out a woman padding through the desert to a well. He saw her needs. He saw her sin. He saw her relational discontent, her religious questions, her longing for something, even if she didn't know exactly what that was. This was not a woman satisfied with her life. Jesus knew how to fix that.

He invited her to ask for water. She did. He invited her to bring her family. She did. He stayed with her people and bolstered her standing in her community, because her relational needs, her community needs, and her heart needs all mattered to him.

So how does this affect me, here in the future? Relationships mean everything, and we live in a fractured society not known for fostering friendships and relationships. Many of us run from person to person looking for intimacy, hoping to be seen and known. We struggle with friendships, marriages, and family relationships. Relationships aren't easy.

Jesus set himself up to be the last water she would ever need, and when he brought up her marriages, he extended the water metaphor to her relationships. Like she came to the well day after day without being truly satisfied, she stood at the marriage altar time and again without being satisfied.

He said he was part of a gift from God, and with him came eternal fulfillment of thirst. Does that also mean that with Jesus we can have eternal fulfillment of our relational needs? Lysa TerKeurst is a well-known author who writes about relationships and boundaries, because our relationships in this world are broken. She points out the need to limit others' access to us, to protect ourselves so we can love well and not find ourselves lost in bad relationships.[3]

Jesus is the relationship with no boundaries. Through the Spirit we have full access to him, and as our Creator he has access to us. With him we are promised overflowing springs. We won't be sucked dry or ignored or lost with him as we can be in other relationships.

And, if I am secure with Jesus, knowing I am seen and understood and loved without measure, I am free to love others lavishly. I am fulfilled in Christ, so human relationships aren't as risky. I don't need as much from them.

Jesus's promise to become for the Samaritan woman a spring welling up to eternal life—that's a promise for you and me, too. If we accept his proposal to love us and care for us, his proposal that we ally with him now and forever, we will find so much fulfillment—relationally and otherwise—that it will overflow from us and reach into eternity. Author William MacDonald says it this way: *All that earth can provide is not sufficient to fill the human heart. But the blessings which Christ provides not only fill the heart, but they are too great for any heart to contain.*[4]

That's a whole lot better than many short marriages with the wrong partners, drinking from the wrong wells.

The invitation is to bring our relational needs to Jesus, to trust him first and foremost, to let him fill us to overflowing. From there our human relationships improve, because nobody can empty us. If Jesus becomes my first friend, my best friend, all my relationships will improve because of it.

I do find myself with one question as this story closes, as we move from those needing a drink to a very large crowd that needed a bite to eat.

Did the woman ever get around to giving Jesus a drink, or was he the only one who served up clean, cool water that day?

95

Filled Baskets and Mother Love

We're taking on another well-known story here, Jesus feeding two crowds. The first feeding, where five thousand are filled, is the only miracle (sans the Resurrection) to appear in all four Gospels. That means it's big and it matters.

Like we did with the Samaritan woman, we're going to dig into a few small details, because a full dive would take us many pages, if not whole books, and covers a lot of ground.

Our specific ground is how Jesus satisfied and fulfilled those he met on the roads, and even more specifically, why he did it. Why does my fulfillment and satisfaction matter to Jesus?

We're going to stick with Mark's version for most of this, and Mark sets the stage with some background. This meal occurred after two important events. First, the disciples went out on mission to heal, cast out demons, and teach. While this was happening, John the Baptist was executed. Some of Jesus's disciples had once followed John, so these men are experiencing joy from their mission and grief from their loss.

In light of these things, Jesus takes his disciples aside for a time of rest. Yes, we can get away, grieve, and rest. Jesus specifically leads his disciples away from the crowds so they can refresh and calm and find peace. That means I can do the same. Disciples don't have to be in action every moment of the day.

The crowds have other ideas, arriving at Jesus's destination before he does. His disciples still need rest, but when he sees the crowd, Mark tells us he had compassion on them, because they were like sheep without a shepherd. So he begins teaching them many things. (Mk. 6:34). Matthew adds that Jesus's compassion led him to heal them, too. (Matt. 14:14). Luke says he welcomed them, taught them, and healed them. (Luke 9:11). John jumps ahead, and he simply says that Jesus saw the crowd and thought about feeding them. (John 6:5)

Before I go any further, I need to go back to my own wrong thinking, because that colors how I read this passage, and it could color how I describe it to you. This passage is rich with Old Testament prophet imagery, Messianic ideas, and lessons, but what I notice first every time I read it is that Jesus did this out of compassion.

He intended to find rest in a quiet place. He got a wild crowd instead. And yet, exasperated Jesus is nowhere to be found. His plans changed, but he welcomed the change. He met this scene with compassion.

Jesus tells us more than once that he does his Father's will, that he doesn't act on his own. I admit sometimes I wonder if he did some of this like a child, doing what a parent asks without his whole heart behind it.

It doesn't take much reading of the Gospels to realize that isn't how Jesus approached anything. He did what God asked because he shares God's love and compassion. They were in full agreement with what needed done. God never asked Jesus to do something and got partial results.

Jesus's compassion is as deep and high and full as God's compassion.

The word used here for compassion refers to the bowel. Strange, right? Where we speak of deep emotions coming from the heart, they spoke of them from the bowel. Jesus's compassion is from deep within, churning his very bowel.

The New Testament was written in Greek, and the Old Testament in Hebrew, so there is no direction translation from one to the other, but there are New Testaments translated partially or fully into Hebrew, and one such translation uses an interesting word to describe Jesus's compassion in this passage.

The Hebrew term is transliterated *racham* or *rachamim*[1], and it can be translated as mercy, but its deeper meaning has to do with the womb. This is the love of a mother toward her child. This has to be one of the deepest, most emotional loves a person can experience, and it moves a person.

Jesus was said more than once to be moved with compassion. Six times in the New Testament he acts after experiencing compassion toward someone or a group. A mother cannot see her child in need and do nothing. This is mama-bear love, protective and fierce.

That's Jesus's love toward us, his lambs. Shepherd love. Lay-down-one's-life love. That was the love that spilled from his heart and actions that day in the crowd.

Okay, back to the story. Jesus is moved, and he changes his plans. He settles this group and teaches and heals.

Then it gets late. The disciples suggest he send them away to eat, but he has another plan in mind.

Mark tells this part this way:

But he answered, "You give them something to eat."
They said to him, "That would take more than half a year's wages! Are we to go and spend that much on bread and give it to them to eat?"
³⁸ "How many loaves do you have?" he asked. "Go and see."
When they found out, they said, "Five—and two fish." Mark 6:37-38

After this, Jesus organizes the group, prays over the food, and lets the disciples distribute it. Everyone eats and is satisfied. Mark specifically says that—they are satisfied. Also, there is food left over.

Jesus satisfies these people out of his own compassion. His bowels and deepest heart were in an uproar over their needs, and he took it upon himself to fill those needs. The Shepherd could do no less.

Three quick things before we shift to see our story through the eyes of those who ate, things that will affect those who ate. First, this happens in Galilee among Jews who knew their Scriptures, and Jesus had just played out two stories. He'd fed people in the wilderness, much like Moses had done with manna. Also, he'd fed a crowd with a few loaves and had food left over, just like Elisha did in 2 Kings 4:42-43 (Elisha fed a hundred men with twenty loaves, and they also ate their fill with food left over.) Jesus is clearly giving off some prophet vibes in this field.

Second, the disciples served. The people didn't stand in a line potluck style. They sat down, and the rabbi's men passed the food to the groups. The disciples, who are weary and grieving, are pulled into this act of service, this amazing, recharging act of service, setting their own needs aside to do it. Many of these men will go on to even greater sacrifice, and some of that understanding of self and sacrifice and the satisfaction of serving—it starts here.

Third, Jesus is showing himself to be the shepherd again, and not just any Shepherd. This is the Shepherd from Ezekiel. Mark says Jesus's compassion sprang from his realization that these people were sheep without a shepherd. That comes from Ezekiel 34:4-5, where God condemns the shepherds of Israel for their poor treatment of their subjects and laments that his sheep are without a shepherd. Jesus aims to remedy that.

Into the crowd

Let's leave Jesus and the disciples and move into the crowd. They heard Jesus was heading to Bethsaida by boat, so they ran ahead. On foot. They moved quickly enough to arrive before Jesus, so they saw him coming in the distance. He'd arrived! They would get to hear the rabbi speak. Maybe he would heal. Oh, so many of them needed healing, and nothing else had helped. Many in the crowd were desperate for health, desperate for blessings and kind words, desperate for teaching that might bring them hope.

As the day passes, Jesus takes time. He didn't heal the whole crowd at once. No, as they'd expected, he took time. He taught with authority. Likely he touched some of them. The process was slow because each one mattered to him, and he continued to deal with them until the sky darkened.

Then the disciples pull Jesus away. Maybe the crowd hears the discourse. Maybe not. But suddenly the disciples are moving through the crowd asking about bread. Then the people are organized into groups and settled in the grass.

This wasn't how a visit with the rabbi was supposed to go. Rabbis didn't feed people. They didn't have grand resources. Their disciples normally didn't have grand resources. So what was about to happen in these groups of people spread all over a huge field near dark?

That's when the disciples brought food. Not just a little food, either. Men ate their fill. Maybe the men ate first. But everyone, from the oldest man to the youngest child, was passed food and ate until satisfied. Not just bread, either. They ate bread and meat. This was truly a feast.

Then things took a dark turn.

Only John, likely the last Gospel writer, gives us insight into the end of this event. Jesus sends the disciples ahead (where later he will walk on the water to meet them) and goes to the mountain, scattering the crowd because he's concerned they will force him to become king.

They hadn't missed the correlation between Jesus and Moses and Elisha. This wasn't simply a prophet in their midst. No, Jesus was winning their trust and dispelling their doubts about his identity and his power, much as we saw in the last chapter, only it was working a little too well, and they were impatient to see this story to its end.

They simply didn't understand exactly how Jesus meant to play out his role as Messiah, and their enthusiasm endangered him and his people.

However, this doesn't quell Jesus's compassion. Eventually he repeats this miracle, only this time the crowd is only four thousand strong and not five.

More hungry souls

So we jump ahead to this second feeding, where Jesus says one of my favorite things in Mark: *I have compassion for these people; they have already been with me three days and have nothing to eat. If I send them home hungry, they will collapse on the way, because some of them have come a long distance.* Mark 8:2-30

As was the case of Jesus's fatigue and thirst in the story of the Samaritan woman, his concern here is real. These people had been with Jesus for three days. Desert heat and lack of food is real. They were honestly in danger if they didn't eat, and Jesus, even though he could fix the problem, felt honest concern. More of that protective mama-bear love.

I never considered the three days before. The first feeding took place after a day. This time, Jesus has been speaking and healing for three days. Did the people camp around him? Were they thinking Exodus, walking the wilderness with God in the lead? Were children racing around like this was a party? Did they fill the field with campfires overnight, telling stories with the disciples about things Jesus had done? Was this a boon to villages around who could sell them food? Or had they depleted the stores of nearby villages like a swarm of locusts?

Whatever the three days felt like, I suspect those involved remembered every moment of it. How could they forget anything about this impromptu retreat with the rabbi who welcomed them, healed them, taught them, and then fed them? One by one, people and their loved ones had the opportunity to sit at Jesus's feet, be the center of his attention, and receive what they needed. Whatever their station, whatever their illness or injury, whatever their need, for those days he satisfied. You know these people found satisfaction, because nobody follows someone into the wilderness for three days without getting something out of it.

Anyway, here on day three food is scarce. In the first Mark passage, where Jesus feeds the five thousand, he tells his disciples to feed the crowd and asks them to determine how many loaves they can find. This time, when he asks how many loaves they have, they have an answer. Sure, this could simply be a condensed telling, or maybe this time the disciples suspected what Jesus meant to do, and they counted loaves ahead of time.

Whatever it was, the three days of healing and speaking ended with another filling meal of both bread and fish where one of the most basic human needs was fulfilled—hunger. After this, Jesus sent the crowd home. It was time for him to move on.

A Shepherd's welcome

In all these accounts Jesus sees the crowds coming. He sees them as a group, and then he welcomes them as individuals. He sees them as sheep, and himself as the Shepherd. They are his responsibility to protect, to feed, to care for, to heal.

The other shepherds in their lives had failed them. The Pharisees, priests, leaders, and ultimately the Romans who ruled over all of them didn't have the best interests of these people at heart. Their leaders were plagued by corruption and the need for power. Even those with spiritual fervor misused it. These people paid too many taxes, missed their national freedom, and didn't see an end in sight.

Ezekiel, years in the past, had written these words of God concerning Israel:

> *'This is what the Sovereign LORD says: Woe to you shepherds of Israel who only take care of yourselves! Should not shepherds take care of the flock? ³ You eat the curds, clothe yourselves with the wool and slaughter the choice animals, but you do not take care of the flock. ⁴ You have not strengthened the weak or healed the sick or bound up the injured. You have not brought back the strays or searched for the lost. You have ruled them harshly and brutally. ⁵ So they were scattered because there was no shepherd, and when they were scattered they became food for all the wild animals. ⁶ My sheep wandered over all the mountains and on every high hill. They were scattered over the whole earth, and no one searched or looked for them.* Ezek. 34:2b-6

This is what Jesus saw. He saw himself as the Shepherd here to collect those sheep, and when he sat them down in the fields and ate with them... I suspect he smiled the entire time. This was the future. One day he will sit and eat with his flock every day. They will never again be scattered or lost or abused. Instead, they will run freely through the fields like the children must have done during those three days in Galilee, free of fears or danger or starvation or abuse.

These two stories are not the only time we read that Jesus was moved by compassion. When he healed the leper in Mark one, and when he healed two blind men in Matthew 20, we learn compassion was his motive. The same with the widow in Luke 7 about to bury her son. In all these cases Jesus felt the gut-churning, mama-bear protective compassion that forced him to act, to heal and love and bring satisfaction and fulfillment to those who could never find these things on their own.

I haven't talked parables before, but two of the best-known parables speak of this same compassion. The father of the prodigal ran to greet his lost son out of this compassion. (Luke 11:20) And the Samaritan tending the injured Jew (Luke 10:33) felt the same.

Jesus told stories that would speak through the ages, and he knew in any time and any place, people would understand this kind of compassion, the love that fulfills needs and fixes problems. This kind of love leads us to seek out the fulfillment and satisfaction of others.

An invitation

We've looked at the crowds, and we've considered what Jesus saw when he looked at them. But what was the invitation? Did Jesus invite anyone into a new story through these events? What does this say about my need for satisfaction?

I see one small but important invitation here. Jesus asks the people to sit in groups. It doesn't sound like much. We don't know if they knew this was for a feast, because when Jesus asked this, he had no more than a few loaves in hand, so it was a stretch to think a feast was coming. However, he said sit, and they sat.

I realize how insignificant this sounds. But let's jump back to Psalm 81, where God is recounting his hopes and disappointments with Israel. Verses 10 and 11 read like this: *I am the LORD your God, who brought you up out of Egypt. Open wide your mouth and I will fill it.* [11] *"But my people would not listen to me; Israel would not submit to me."*

God told the people of Israel on multiple occasions that if they obeyed, they would be satisfied. He promised good crops and safe homes. Wine and fields and livestock and peace. Everything good would be theirs.

They said no.

So when Jesus asks these people at the end of a long day to sit… They are hungry. They are tired. They are excited, because each of them brought something away from the day, either renewed health or greater understanding of their spiritual situation, but they are reaching their end. The wilderness isn't safe for crowds without food.

And then the rabbi, who seems to have no food, who has been in discussion with his disciples for a few minutes and sends those disciples polling the crowd for food, doesn't send them away. He doesn't suggest they take care of themselves and head to the villages for a meal. No, he has them sit in groups in the grass.

They say yes. I wonder if any left, unsure and hungry and thinking they had to take care of themselves. Or had Jesus once again proven himself so trustworthy that all of them settled, curious about what might happen next?

I started this section talking about our sprints from thing to thing to satisfy ourselves. Media, phones, romances, money—we look everywhere to satisfy ourselves. I admit I run ahead. Or I did. As I've gotten older, I've slowed down. When things feel like they're falling apart, and Jesus is standing in front of me with no food in hand asking me to sit and open my mouth, I'm more likely to sit and open my mouth.

Because only he truly knows how to satisfy. He does it with lovingkindness. He does it by offering rest and refreshment. He does it with rain and sun in season and food for every living thing.

I don't have to run the maze of this world, tucking into every nook and cranny looking for what will fill me up. I simply need to step onto Jesus's road of fulfillment. There I will have opportunity to sit at his feet and look into his eyes. Sometimes I will sit in the grass with no idea what's coming next, but I can be assured that what comes next is for my good.

Jesus saw his sheep lost and scattered, and he longed to gather them and satisfy them. As Psalm 23 says, he provides green pastures and still waters. A rod and staff will protect us.

The invitation here is to wait, to listen, to take Jesus's direction even if it doesn't quite make sense. And in doing so, we don't try to find satisfaction in the wrong things, drinking out of the wrong wells. It's simple. And yet it can take a lifetime to put it into practice.

Waiting on Jesus takes trust, like we saw in the last section. Trust and obedience and a life of satisfaction work together.

So where don't you trust? Where do you doubt? I've asked it before, but a whole lot hangs on the answer. Now add to it the question of where you are in the maze. Are you trapped on your phone? Chasing romance down every dark alley? Are you worrying about real, honest needs like rent money or affordable medicine?

We have needs, and we have desires, and God knows that. But oh, when he says to sit down, stop running, and wait for him to fill those empty places... This takes faith and trust and prayer on our part. At least it does on my part. The disciples saw Jesus feed five thousand people, and yet they seemed a little surprised when he did it again with four thousand.

I do the same thing. Sure, God's brought me through many valleys before. But maybe this time I'll reach for him and he won't reach back.

Through his dealings with Peter and a woman at a well and two hungry crowds, we see that Jesus reaches back. Often he reaches out first. His compassion for us won't allow him to do otherwise. He will supply all our needs according to his riches. Our final need will be to close our eyes here and open them in the next world that awaits us, but until then, he meets our human needs.

Wait on Jesus. Don't run the maze, but settle in the grass with wide eyes seeing what he will do. His provision might surprise you.

From here we continue down the road to land on a story I love about two grieving, confused people wandering down a road after Jesus's death, and how Jesus quelled their fears and grief with the simple addition of information.

Yes, we move on to Jesus's desire to satisfy our curiosity and God-given need to know about the world around us as we walk the road to Emmaus.

Delighted by Understanding

You're probably familiar with the idea of *need-to-know* information, especially if you watch military thrillers. The higher-ups don't tell their underlings more than is required to do their job. The underlings often fight this. We want to know more than we need to know.

We hear it in media, too, the idea that *I have the right to know*. We apply it to everything. The right to know what our favorite celebrities are up to. The right to know all the government's secrets.

We hate secrets.

Satan used this against the first people on the planet. How did he tempt Eve? He told her God had secrets, and she had the right to know.

The reality is God wants to share his secrets with us. He's given us a good dose of curiosity. We crave knowledge. We don't like to be in the dark, and we're not good at blind obedience.

That's okay, because it's clear in the Bible that blind obedience was never God's plan for us. Sin cuts us off from God, but through Jesus we are restored, and God is again close and shares with us.

Jesus shows us this clearly in the story of two men on the road to Emmaus. It's one of the more humorous tales in the Bible, and it shows Jesus's desire to equip us with everything we need—and want—to know to honor and follow him.

To set the stage, Luke 24:13-35 takes place on Easter Sunday. The women have gone to the tomb. In this telling, there's no mention of them seeing Jesus, so perhaps they've kept that to themselves for the moment. Two disciples, not among the twelve, leave Jerusalem, lost, confused, and heartbroken. They were so sure Jesus was the Messiah, but it didn't turn out like they'd expected. Then add to it the women's crazy story that Jesus was alive… Their grief sent them where grief sends a lot of us, straight home.

They have a seven-mile walk, and as they walk they discuss the Passover events that had just happened. Along the way a stranger sidles up next to them. This isn't strange. Many Jews wandered home after Passover, and many of them walked together. In a land where hospitality reigned and travel was often hot, dusty, and undertaken on foot, a little company was welcome.

Luke lets us in on the irony from the beginning. He's definitely writing this to make us smile. And why not? We just read a heartbreaking story of Jesus's death. I don't know about you, but even though I know the outcome, I struggle to read about the crucifixion. It hurts to my bones.

Maybe it hurt to the bones of his readers, too, so Luke lightens the mood with his telling of this tale. Who knows?

Jesus asks them what they're discussing, and they stop, somewhat stunned. One of them is shocked that anyone coming from Jerusalem could be so clueless. Jesus's crucifixion seems to be the story of the day. What rock was this man living under?

Jesus presses, and they tell him. I cannot imagine this story without Jesus hiding a smile. This is that classic trope of someone thought dead attending his own funeral. Jesus listens as these two followers explain Jesus's ministry in their own words. He hears their confusion, their heartbreak, and their frustration.

He calls them foolish. Yes, it seems harsh. Maybe it was meant to be harsh. But he's also still in the role of stranger, not their beloved rabbi, and teachers can be harsh when faced with clueless students. In this role of teacher, he explains to them what the Old Testament has to say about the Messiah. The seven-mile walk likely takes two to three hours, so Jesus can cover a lot of territory.

When they arrive, they ask the stranger to stay. It's getting late, and hospitality protocols say to invite the man to stay. He acts like he isn't going to accept—also hospitality protocols—and then stays.

Next he breaks bread. *Not* hospitality protocols. This man is not the host. But the pair seems to realize he's someone special. He's educated and speaks with authority, so they let him serve.

We readers are waiting to see what happens next. We are reminded of the feeding of the five thousand and the Last Supper. We know the identity of this man. We see the symbolism here, and we're at the edge of our seats wondering when this pair will figure it out.

The breaking of bread seals the deal. They realize who's been with them today, and when they do, Jesus is gone. It's implied that both their inability to recognize him and then their open eyes was all divinely appointed, but it's still a satisfying reveal topped off with a miraculous disappearance.

Then in verse thirty-two, one of them says something important. *Were not our hearts burning within us while he talked with us on the road and opened the Scriptures to us?*

They didn't know who Jesus was, and yet what he said made their hearts burn. Was it because of the messenger, or was it the message? I'm going to hedge my bets and say both, but I'm also going to say that because we now have the Spirit, the truths about Jesus in the Bible burn in our hearts, too.

Those truths increase our understanding. Jesus didn't want this pair in the dark (I'm not going to call them men, because some commentators suggest this might be Cleopas and his wife.). They needed to understand what had happened because they had a job to do. It's the same job all of us have to do, advancing the Kingdom. And to advance it, we have to understand it.

Some distant illumination

We're going to back away from the wandering pair and do some bouncing through the Bible. I love bouncing through the Bible. The idea that God wants to share with us isn't only here. It's all over the place. Themes of understanding abound. It's tied to wisdom, because wisdom comes from understanding. It has to do with how God views us, and it has implications for how we live our lives.

Finally, we will see that knowledge and understanding fulfill us. We are satisfied when things make sense. We are satisfied when those who love us trust us with their secrets.

So, allow me to back away from Luke before we ask our seen and invited questions, and let's do a little wandering of our own.

Big surprise, I want to start in the Psalms. Psalm 119, which is all about knowing Scripture, talks about this more than once, so I snagged one verse which says *The unfolding of your words gives light; it gives understanding to the simple* Ps. 119: 130

True understanding, true knowledge, is in the words of God. It lights our way and moves from simple to wise.

Then we have Psalm 25:14. In the NIV Bible version, the verse reads like this: *The LORD confides in those who fear him; he makes his covenant known to them.*

That first phrase is translated various ways in different translations, and here are two, first the International Children's Bible and then the Revised Standard Version: *The Lord tells his secrets to those who respect him.* And *The friendship of the Lord is for those who fear him.*

This is not the picture of a God who makes difficult laws and demands blind obedience. If ever that has been your view of God, let these words convince you otherwise. We're friends who get God's secrets.

Now we bounce to Paul, who says in Colossions 2: *My goal is that they may be encouraged in heart and united in love, so that they may have the full riches of complete understanding, in order that they may know the mystery of God, namely, Christ, in whom are hidden all the treasures of wisdom and knowledge.* Colossians 2:2-3

Understanding, knowledge, and wisdom are treasures. They lead us to understand Jesus, because he is the basis of reality. You want to know everything worth knowing? Look to Jesus.

Okay, back to the Old Testament, this time to Isaiah 32. Here Isaiah speaks of a glorious future for God's people. He describes a land of justice and righteousness, a good and safe place to live.

Then in verse 4 he says *The fearful heart will know and understand...*

Did you catch that? Fear can come from not understanding. We know God doesn't want us afraid. We know faith in him is the key to us becoming fearless, but we've also seen Jesus demonstrate God's works to us to convince us.

We are asked to believe based on something real. Understanding and knowledge are some of these real things. As we understand more, we fear less.

Consequences of knowledge

Let's head back to our pair on the road, although we're going to bounce again after this. This passage simply cries out for some bouncing, because the lesson here has such a broad scope.

I once sat in on a discussion of this passage, and someone said they wished the conversation among these three had been recorded. I think it is. After Jesus disappeared, this pair returned to Jerusalem post haste. Yes, they had to proclaim that Jesus was alive. I'm sure that was their first goal. But they also shared what he'd told them. I think we see it all over the place. The gospel writers make many allusions to Old Testament passages about Jesus. Paul does it. The writer of Hebrews does it. I suspect some of that came from here.

Because we know Jesus gave this teaching, we can trust it. It didn't come from human minds. When Matthew subtly compares Jesus to Moses, he had that interpretation on good authority. When John starts his gospel alluding to Genesis, he knows what he's talking about.

Jesus says the pair is foolish not to see this, but then he explains it. It's important that they know the details, and it's important that they pass it forward. And, once he reveals himself, those words take on deeper meaning. They make the heart burn with their truth and their power, and the writers and teachers from that day forward pass the information down the line.

Seen and Invited

So, let's take on our questions before we bounce away again, because these questions will set the course of our bouncing. What did Jesus see when he found this pair on the road?

He saw disciples. His heart went out to them, because these were his lambs. Many of them were still in Jerusalem lamenting together, but this pair had gotten away. Grief was sending them home, away from the flock. They were going to be part of a bigger story, and that meant they needed to let go of their grief, gain some understanding, and return to the fold.

He saw two people who played no other role in this story. They're not the twelve. One doesn't even get a name. Some suggest Cleopas is named because the early readers of Luke's gospel might have heard of him, so maybe he plays a further role. But eleven men close to Jesus are in the upper room grieving together, and Jesus chooses this unknown pair to carry some really vital information to the rest.

Because Jesus knew them. He cared for them. Their role had been small before, historically speaking, but it wasn't small now. Maybe the pair had great memories. Maybe they had skills writing, and they returned to Jerusalem and wrote some of this down. We don't have any idea why Jesus chose them as the recipients of this very important conversation, but he did. People who seem to be lesser players in the kingdom aren't lesser at all. I don't have to feel important in the story to get important roles to play, and what feels like a small role might have grand eternal consequences.

So he spoke with them, taught them, stunned them, and indirectly sent them back to the group, where some sharing happened. Those in Jerusalem welcomed them and told them Peter had seen Jesus. Was this before or after Jesus spoke with the Emmaus pair? We'll never know. They shared stories, got excited, and talked each other down from the ledges. Now that they had Jesus's explanations and understood the resurrection, I suspect they told story after story about what they'd seen and heard from Jesus over the past three years, laughing as it all became clear.

Possibly during this conversation Jesus appears again to the group, and he opens all their minds. After this, the sharing would start anew. Imagine the rolling eyes and slapping of foreheads when Jesus's more cryptic words weren't cryptic any longer.

Jesus doesn't give a direct invitation in this passage. He disappears before dinner. But look what his visit with this pair does for them. They want to know more. The conversation isn't over. Now that they know some, they want to know it all. Jesus invites them to keep looking, to keep seeking knowledge. Because their hearts burn, they want to share what they know. Maybe they head straight back that night. Maybe it's later. But it isn't long. When our spirits are roused and instructed by God's spirit, we want to share.

So the invitation, brought about by the emotions Jesus evoked, is for them to dig deeper and share. It sends them back into community and out of their lonely grief.

I don't have stories about my time with Jesus to share with others, not like these people did. I wasn't there in Jerusalem. Instead, I dig using the written gospels. I scour what those eyewitnesses left for me: the gospels and the letters. And that burning in my heart when I hear these words? That's still for me, as is the desire to share with others what I learn.

Spirit promptings

This leads us to another quick trip through the Bible. Jesus promised us knowledge and understanding through the Spirit. I might not have personal stories about Jesus's time on earth, but I have the promptings of the Spirit. Listen to Jesus's promise to us concerning the Spirit:

But the Advocate, the Holy Spirit, whom the Father will send in my name, will teach you all things and will remind you of everything I have said to you. [27] Peace I leave with you; my peace I give you. I do not give to you as the world gives. Do not let your hearts be troubled and do not be afraid. John 14:26-27

Then let's back up and learn a little more about the Spirit. Isaiah 11 is about Jesus and his future reign. But what we read about the Spirit—this same Spirit is mine. Jesus promised Him to me. Isaiah says:

The Spirit of the LORD will rest on him—
  the Spirit of wisdom and of understanding,
  the Spirit of counsel and of might,
  the Spirit of the knowledge and fear of the LORD—
and he will delight in the fear of the LORD. Isaiah 11:1-3

I can expect wisdom, understanding, knowledge, fear of the

Lord, and more, because Jesus promised the Spirit. This also means I can expect to delight in the fear of the Lord.

With the Spirit comes knowledge. With knowledge comes delight. With delight comes fulfillment, because most of us run from thing to thing in this world seeking fulfillment, and one way we experience fulfillment is through delight. When we are delighted and happy, we feel satisfied.

I'm going to toss out a few verses and let you draw your own conclusions. Pay close attention to the concepts of delight and thirst.

Take delight in the LORD, and he will give you the desires of your heart. Psalm 37:4

Blessed is the one... whose delight is in the law of the LORD,
and who meditates on his law day and night.
That person is like a tree planted by streams of water,
which yields its fruit in season
and whose leaf does not wither—
whatever they do prospers. Psalm 1:1-3

You, God, are my God, earnestly I seek you; I thirst for you, my whole being longs for you, in a dry and parched land where there is no water. Psalm 63:1

"Whoever believes in me, as Scripture has said, rivers of living water will flow from within them." By this he meant the Spirit, whom those who believed in him were later to receive. Up to that time the Spirit had not been given, since Jesus had not yet been glorified. John 7:38-39

I am the Alpha and the Omega, the Beginning and the End. To the thirsty I will give water without cost from the spring of the water of life. Revelation 21:6b

Empowered words

Jesus gave the pair on the road their answers while hiding his identity because soon they and all the disciples would be asked to proclaim Jesus based on words alone. Jesus himself would no longer be here to perform miracles. It was down to the words.

But he sent us the Spirit to empower those words. We long for our thirsts to be quenched and to find delight in this dark world. Jesus says that happens through the Spirit, and one of the Spirit's great vehicles is the Word of God.

We know fulfillment and satisfaction by scouring the Word for knowledge and letting the Spirit use it to give us direction, for counsel and might, and to draw closer to God.

We know fulfillment by admitting everything we run for here leaves us parched. I mean, how often do you step away from social media or a phone game feeling truly full? We are a culture of people who overeat, binge on shows, and devour and argue news like it will fix the problems of the universe.

Admit you're parched. Admit you're grieving and longing for home. Fill your heart with Jesus and his words so the Spirit can burn in your heart and delight your spirit and quench your thirsts.

I leave the Emmaus pair with a verse from John that Jesus spoke on his final pre-crucifixion night: *I no longer call you servants, because a servant does not know his master's business. Instead, I have called you friends, for everything that I learned from my Father I have made known to you.* John 15:15

Because of the Spirit, we are Jesus's friends. He wants us curious, and then he wants to satisfy.

Final thoughts on fulfillment

Personally, I am prone to days of restlessness. Some days nothing satisfies—not food, not entertainment, not family or friends. I'm not sure what triggers those days, but they never last long, which is good, because discontentment is powerfully disabling. The quest to fill all my needs, especially when I don't know what those needs are, can lead me down very shady alleys and off the safe roads.

For some, the never-ending quest for something new and exciting and stimulating is much greater, and the thought of anchoring one's life in religion… They can't imagine anything worse.

But we saw in this section that true adventures happen on God's road of satisfaction. Jesus satisfies relational needs, physical needs, and mental needs. His desire is for our lives to be full and exciting. He puts challenges in our paths and asks us to become more than we ever thought we could be. And he doesn't leave us to do it alone. He gave us the Spirit to enable us to live this full life he desires for us.

He sees you, understands the empty spots in your heart, and fills them in creative ways only He can, unique ways made just for you.

Now we jump to another road, one that's too quiet and has dangerous shadows lurking at the edges. The road of isolation is a road where many fall prey to the Enemy of God. Fortunately, the Shepherd walks this road—and invites us to walk this road at his side—rescuing at-risk sheep and leading them to the road of community. And that's where we journey next.

Section Four: The Silent Road of Isolation

Community. If you've travelled this world very long, you know it's not easy to find community. People are a mess. And yet, God makes it clear we're to live within groups. Churches, villages, families—all have places in the kingdom. When we rub each other the wrong way, we also rub off hard edges. We learn from one another. We keep each other going.

Jesus touched individuals on the roads, but often he returned these broken souls back into the arms of a community.

We've seen some of this. The woman at the well returned to her village, and Jesus spent time within that village for three days. The bleeding woman, unable to live within her religious community because of her uncleanness, was shown in front of witnesses to be healed and ready to resume community life again.

Being isolated is dangerous. In 1 Peter 5, Peter speaks to the elders, warning them to protect their flocks, to live out their lives together in community with humility. Verse 8 says *Be alert and of sober mind. Your enemy the devil prowls around like a roaring lion looking for someone to devour.* Lions don't take on whole flocks of sheep. They come for the stragglers, the unhealthy, those on the fringes. Peter warns the leaders to keep their flock tightly knitted together and healthy so there are no stragglers to pick off.

Jesus demonstrates this, too, restoring people to community. We're going to venture onto the road of isolation and watch him set three lost souls back into the arms of community, protecting them, loving them, and giving them full lives they couldn't get on their own.

No Strength of Her Own

There are many reasons a person might find herself without community. Sin separates us from our people. Gossip and slander do the same. Sometimes we do it to ourselves, and sometimes we are victims. In this story in Luke, a woman finds herself outside her community through nobody's fault. She did nothing wrong. Her community did nothing wrong. Instead, the entire culture around her isolated her, and when Jesus came upon her, he had to do something dramatic to restore her.

The passage is short, simple, and amazing, so we'll read through it before we start:

> *Soon afterward, Jesus went to a town called Nain, and his disciples and a large crowd went along with him.* ¹² *As he approached the town gate, a dead person was being carried out—the only son of his mother, and she was a widow. And a large crowd from the town was with her.* ¹³ *When the Lord saw her, his heart went out to her and he said, "Don't cry."*
>
> ¹⁴ *Then he went up and touched the bier they were carrying him on, and the bearers stood still. He said, "Young man, I say to you, get up!"* ¹⁵ *The dead man sat up and began to talk, and Jesus gave him back to his mother.*
>
> ¹⁶ *They were all filled with awe and praised God. "A great prophet has appeared among us," they said. "God has come to help his people."* ¹⁷ *This news about Jesus spread throughout Judea and the surrounding country.*
> Luke 7:11-17

At this point in Luke, Jesus is making waves in the north. His home base seems to be Capernaum, and Nain, where he meets this woman, is likely a few miles from Capernaum. He travels with a crowd, for he has been teaching and healing for a while.

So we have two crowds meeting just outside the gates of Nain. One is loud with joy and praise. The other is loud with grief. They stop, and the head of one group makes eye contact with the head of the other. The differences would have been humorous if they weren't so sad. The widow's son is lying on a bier, carried to his final place of rest, when the area's favored son Jesus is alive, standing on his own two feet, celebrated, heading toward great things.

Her son might have been headed for great things. Likely he was headed for humble things, caring for his mother and living in his small town. Except he had been cut off, and this woman was alone.

The Shepherd's heart

Jesus's reaction to this woman is another of the gut-wrenching, pain-to-the-bowel reactions. He sees the deep truths of this situation. Not that losing a son isn't bad enough, but this woman is a widow, and this son is her only son.

This woman has lost her family. She's lost her status, income, and community. Likely she lost her son this very same day, for in this culture the dead were buried right away. She'd wakened that morning with a son and a future. She planned to go to bed that night—probably not to sleep, for sleep is still days away in her grief— with no son and no future.

And Jesus feels her loss and her hopelessness down into his bowels.

He approaches, and both crowds must have to stop. Did the Jesus crowd go silent in deference to the mourning crowd? Do they look to Jesus with expectation? With puzzlement? Just a day ago he healed a centurion's servant from a distance, but he doesn't seem to be keeping his distance here.

No, he walks right up to the woman and tells her not to cry.

It's easy to say those words when someone is in pain. We want to offer comfort and hope, but what can we say or do? We know we can't stop grief with those simple words, but we speak them anyway.

When Jesus spoke them, they weren't words of comfort. They were a hint of things to come.

Again, I wonder about his crowd. We don't know how often he raised the dead. We have three recorded events, but Jesus lived more unrecorded days than recorded. We also don't know if this was the first time he did it. However, the crowd knows Jesus does out-of-the-ordinary things. I suspect the area got quiet as everyone waited to see what would happen next.

The man was carried on a bier, and Jesus touched it. Yes, we deal with uncleanness again. Maybe the crowd was used to this. Maybe they were surprised. The widow's crowd was likely surprised. Whether they knew Jesus's identity or not, this man was leading a crowd. He was *someone*. We mentioned his dress might give him away as a religious leader, but maybe he was simply someone important. Whatever he was, touching biers of the dead isn't a normal thing for an important stranger to do.

Then he speaks directly to the young man, telling him to get up. The man sits up and talks, clearly alive and in his right mind, fully restored. Jesus then gives him back to his mother.

I wish I had a camera for that moment. Her grief spoke to his heart and led him to this young man's side. Now he looks her in the eyes and makes it clear to her that all is well. This man is alive. She now has family again. She has status in her community again. The woman who a few minutes ago was as alone as a person can be now belongs again.

I wonder if she hugged her son. Maybe she hugged Jesus. I suspect two crowds, each loud for their own purposes, were now loud for a single purpose, joy. Luke tells us they praised God, and Israelites didn't praise God quietly. Many voices joined. We read two of the statements they gave—that a prophet had appeared and that God had come close—but I suspect there were more things said. What had started as a funeral had become a party.

But that moment when Jesus gives her son to her… Maybe he gave the boy a hand to stand up. Maybe he touched the woman and then the man, indicating their togetherness. Maybe he stood back and let the scene play out from the side, and the woman nodded at him, tears in her eyes.

She hadn't expected this joy. Possibly she hadn't expected to experience joy ever again. But here she stands as a stranger looks at her with love and restores her life to her.

I love this simple story. What I love most is its spontaneity. Sure, Jesus knew what was coming. But nobody here asked for his help. No faith was required. Jesus responded to his own compassion. He saw something that touched him, and he fixed it. It's not the first or last time, but it touches me down to my own bowels every time it happens.

This is the Shepherd, surrounding the authority of the king and working from compassion and love.

The Prophet's authority

Of course, there's more to the story. There's always more to the story. Not that Jesus reviving this young man and restoring his mother to her community and family isn't enough—it is enough. But Jesus wasn't on the road alone. He did this in sight of two crowds, so he used his limited time to speak to more than this man and his mother.

Jesus lives out Old Testament stories often, showing that he is the culmination of what happened then. Everything before him pointed to him. This story is no different. Here Jesus enacts two stories about prophets. In 1 Kings 17 the prophet Elijah is staying with a woman, and her son dies. Elijah calls to God for help, stretches himself over the boy three times, and restores his life. As Jesus does in Luke, Elijah *gave him to his mother*. The woman's response? She suddenly believes Elijah is a man of God who speaks the words of God. (1 Kings 17:17-24) Pretty much the same reaction of the crowds here.

Then in 2 Kings 4:32-37 Elijah's successor Elisha does the same thing. He lays across a dead boy, and the boy warms up. Then he does it again, and the boy lives. In Luke the young man talks. In 2 Kings the young man sneezes. Both are delightful signs that life has returned.

So Jesus is playing out scenes from the prophets. Only he doesn't have to lie over someone multiple times. He has more authority than the prophets of old. He simply touches the plank upon which this man is carried and speaks to him, and his life is restored.

The crowd doesn't miss the symbolism. Jesus is best known at this point as a prophet, like John is also a prophet (he's still alive at this time). Jesus hushes people who call him Messiah, needing to stay alive until the right time, but he doesn't hesitate to let himself be known as a prophet, someone who acts with God's power and speaks with God's tongue.

For those who witnessed this—and this wasn't done in any kind of private setting—the action solidifies what they already knew, that Jesus had the authority of God on his side. They spread the word far.

Seen and Invited

Jesus saw this woman from afar, leading her sorrowful party to a grave. He saw this woman's isolation. He saw her hopelessness, her loneliness, her grief. He saw a young man gone too soon, a man who had more to do. Jesus gave him back the life he was meant to have, because I think we all agree his death was an event only meant to last a day.

Jesus invited the man to get up. Pretty big thing to ask a dead man. But then he gave the man the power to obey. He invited the woman to take her son back, to go back to her position as a mother, as a villager. He invites her back into the life she lost. I suspect she didn't hesitate to take him up on that invitation.

He invited the crowds to believe he had come from God. He invited them to trust more fully, to see God in him. No, they didn't understand he *was* God at this point, but they're getting closer, and honestly, Jesus isn't in a hurry for them to connect those particular dots yet. It's enough to be a prophet.

The power of a borrowed bell

So our normal question stands. What does this mean today? Does Jesus still crash into lives unexpected, feel pain at a gut level, and offer help?

Yes. I experienced it this very Easter Sunday. I was going to be in church alone. Much of my family doesn't attend church at this point, and those who do had responsibilities during worship that week, so

I was sitting in the pew alone. As I sat, I remembered the days when my young family all sat with me, when they seemed to believe. I let myself wallow in regrets, and I expected to weep my way through the whole service. It wouldn't have been the first time.

Out of the blue, a married couple said they were going to sit with me. I knew this pair, but never once had they sat with me. For the most part, they sit alone a few rows ahead of me, but the woman asked to sit with me, and of course I said yes. I was out on the edge of the flock that day, and God didn't want me picked off. No, that Easter morning I was to be dragged back into community and protected.

Our church celebrates Easter by ringing bells during the service—we Anglicans like our celebrations—and this woman put a bell in my hand. She had no idea whatsoever what had been in my heart that day or how much I'd needed company. God simply put it into her head to sit with me. Earlier that morning, God had put it in her head to grab an extra bell. I'm sure she had no idea what was coming, that those two simple acts were her being Jesus's compassionate heart and loving touch toward me.

Instead of weeping my way through a service, I rang my bell, raised my arms with my friend, and celebrated down to my toes. I think it's the first time I ever found my arms in the air with praise. My family still wasn't there, nor were those regrets laid to rest. But Jesus saw to it that I had a place in community, that I wasn't alone. He was going to look out for me, to keep me from being picked off at the edge of the flock, and he will continue to look out for me.

Not only that, if he can fill needs I never asked to have filled, how much more can he hear and fill needs I cry out for, like the eventual restoration of my family, currently little more than dead bodies on their biers being walked out of the village of Nain. His care for me that day restored hope for his care extending to more days, when the hope I had was waning.

What about you? Where has Jesus crashed into your life and done things you never expected him to do? When has he given you a sense of community and belonging? Ask God to bring those to mind so you can celebrate and praise like the crowds who saw the little

Nain family restored. Or like I did with my borrowed bell one Easter morning.

You have a role in this story

What makes this section different than some of the others is that we can help Jesus restore people to community. The Peter passage at the beginning of this section was all about the elders preventing their people from being picked off. All of us can do that.

Who lives on the fringe? Who can't get back on his own? Who's living outside the norm, treading water with no hope of a life preserver? What can you do to help?

I'll admit right now that this section makes me cringe. I live in the country. I struggle to make my way into town for church and groceries, let alone to rescue people who might be lonely targets for Satan. I'm happy to write this and tell all of you to snatch the lost, but... Right. I don't always practice what I preach.

For a while, when I lived in town, my son and I helped feed people once a month. Many of these people were homeless. Some were single parents. Some were there because of their own mistakes, and some through no fault of their own, like those with mental illness or who were abandoned by families.

I loved to pour coffee. I know it sounds crazy, but nothing made me happier than filling foam cups with coffee. They'd hold out their cups, some with a smile, some with a frown, and I would take the cup, fill it—I wasn't confident enough in my pouring skills to pour it while they held the cup, afraid of burning someone—and then place it back in their hands.

Our hands brushed. Many who live alone don't get human touch. But on those days I would brush hands with people. They had a moment to feel human skin. For that moment, they were warm, their needs were met, and they were part of community. Some of them came every day. This was where they belonged. The woman who ran this place had limitless compassion for these people, and they knew that. I didn't help often enough to know their names, but some did.

I played a role in that restorative community. Right now, I don't have a role like that, and I need to find one. Writing this to you, while it may be what God wants in part, isn't enough. I have to find ways to use my particular gifts and skills and passions to protect the fringes of Jesus's flock. You probably need to do the same.

Find those who are walking alone, without community at their sides. We're about to see two more situations where people find themselves alone, so maybe hearing their stories will give you a better idea where to look for the isolated.

Jesus felt down to his bowels the sorrow of the widow. I want to feel that, too. For now, while our hearts and minds ponder this story, we walk further on to one of greatest Sunday school stories ever told, a story of a little man who hid in a tree and found himself with a completely changed life.

When the Crowd Won't Forgive

Every child in Sunday School knows Zacchaeus, the short tax collector who ran ahead of Jesus's entourage and hid in a tree to watch Jesus pass. To a child, the idea of someone short enough not to be able to see over the crowd is familiar, and for Jesus to stop and call this little man into his presence—how delightful that is to a child, who can feel small and outside.

As adults, we have a lot to learn from this man. As we dig into this story we find some powerful lessons in Jesus's response to Zacchaeus, the crowd's response to Zacchaeus, and Zacchaeus's response to Jesus's actions towards him. Luke tells the story this way:

> *Jesus entered Jericho and was passing through. ² A man was there by the name of Zacchaeus; he was a chief tax collector and was wealthy. ³ He wanted to see who Jesus was, but because he was short he could not see over the crowd. ⁴ So he ran ahead and climbed a sycamore-fig tree to see him, since Jesus was coming that way.*
> *⁵ When Jesus reached the spot, he looked up and said to him, "Zacchaeus, come down immediately. I must stay at your house today." ⁶ So he came down at once and welcomed him gladly.*
> *⁷ All the people saw this and began to mutter, "He has gone to be the guest of a sinner."*
> *⁸ But Zacchaeus stood up and said to the Lord, "Look, Lord! Here and now I give half of my possessions to the poor, and if I have cheated anybody out of anything, I will pay back four times the amount."*
> *⁹ Jesus said to him, "Today salvation has come to this house, because this man, too, is a son of Abraham. ¹⁰ For the Son of Man came to seek and to save the lost."* Luke 19:1-10

To set the stage, this happens late in Jesus's ministry. Jesus is on his way to Jerusalem to die, and we get two stories in Luke about him passing through Jericho. The first involves a blind man who calls to Jesus from the side of the road. The crowd tries to quiet the man, but he won't stay quiet. He calls again, and Jesus stops, asks him what he wants, and heals him.

Possibly while this is happening, Zacchaeus, a city tax collector, engages in some strongly non-tax-collector behavior. He runs ahead of the crowd and climbs into a tree. We're told it's a sycamore-fig tree, which means it has huge leaves, so his climb serves two purposes. It gives him the height required to see, and it lets him hide, because no self-respecting tax collector hoists his robe, runs through the streets, and sits in a tree to hear a wandering rabbi, even one as famous as Jesus.

What drove Zacchaeus into the tree? Luke gives us two pieces of background on Zacchaeus: he was a chief tax collector (read *Important Man Who Wouldn't Be Caught Dead Running and Hiding in a Tree*), and he was wealthy. As far as Zacchaeus's goal that day, Luke simply tells us he wanted to see who Jesus was, and he was too short. But for a high-status man to run and hide indicates a powerful want to see Jesus. Something in this man's soul was stirring. The need to see Jesus, whether Zacchaeus understood it or not, had gotten strong enough to force him to take unusual action.

As Jesus gets closer, one of two things happens. One possibility is that only Jesus knew Zacchaeus was in that tree. He knew God had a supernatural appointment with this tax collector, and Jesus steps right up to the tree, looks up, and surprises everyone when he calls a man's name, and a short tax collector climbs down into their sight. Knowing a man's name without an introduction is a very prophet-like thing to do.

Another possibility is that Zacchaeus wasn't hidden well, and everyone saw him. Remember how the crowd responded to the blind man? They told him to be quiet. Interactive crowds are quite the norm in our gospel stories. Chances are the crowd would have something to say to the unpopular tax collector caught sitting in a tree, too. Would they jeer him? Did they want him to get away from their beloved rabbi? Did they think Jesus would want nothing to do with a man who regularly cheated Jews, as tax collectors were known to do?

> The need to see Jesus, whether Zacchaeus understood it or not, had gotten strong enough to force him to take unusual action.

If this was the case, Jesus wasn't the first one to call Zacchaeus by name. No, others were giving the small man trouble, and Jesus uses this moment not only to call to Zacchaeus's heart, but also to speak to a crowd that judged a man by his vocation and reputation.

Remember, what Jesus does is seldom private. Jesus uses almost every interaction to speak to individuals, disciples, and the crowds. This moment may have been for the crowd as much as the tax collector.

Jesus calls the man down, speaking his name and telling him he must come to his house today. Now who was acting out of character? People begged teachers and leaders to come and stay with them. Teachers and leaders rarely chose men out of a crowd, or out of a tree, and invited themselves for dinner.

When Jesus looks up and says the man's name, the crowd may think they know the next part of the story. Jesus is about to dress down the tax collector and stand up for the little guys. That's what Jesus did. He took care of the lesser people. A tax collector was low in status among the Jews, but in society, this was a man of wealth and high standing, a man respected by the Romans who controlled Judea. He worked for the bad guys, and they expected he would get a very wise, cutting reprimand from the rabbi, the same kind of thing Jesus gave to the Pharisees.

Imagine the silence when, instead of scolding Zacchaeus, Jesus says he has to go to his house today. For a moment, every head tilts.

What? Eating in the home of an outsider wasn't what a Jewish holy leader did. What about protocol? Many worthy men lived in town. Couldn't Jesus have eaten with a synagogue leader? That would have made more sense.

But no. Jesus tells Zacchaeus, the tax man in the tree, that he must eat with him. And how does Zacchaeus respond? He comes straight out of that tree and welcomes him. Jesus looked up, saw this man, invited him to take action, and Zacchaeus gladly welcomed Jesus in return.

Two stories, one Shepherd

Let's pause the story right here. Jesus has just spoken with two very different men on his way through Jericho. A blind man is quieted by the crowd because he doesn't belong, and Jesus heals him. After this the crowd praises God. The blind man's status and future were just improved, and they knew that was a good thing, even though they'd wanted him to hush and leave Jesus alone a moment before.

Now Jesus offers kindness to a tax collector. Does the crowd praise God for this? Nope. They don't understand what Jesus is doing. They don't see that Zacchaeus's heart was changing, a change that drove him into a tree. They don't see the desire to get close to Jesus at any cost, a desire that Zacchaeus himself might not have understood. Why did this little man want so badly to get close to a man he didn't know? Did he hope to see miracles? Did he need something new to believe in? Was wealth getting old? Was he tired of not fitting into Jewish religious life because of his job?

We can't answer any of those things. We can guess, and we can wonder, but all we know is that the man was stirred to odd behavior by his curiosity, and now he's standing in front of a hostile crowd beaming his delight at the chance to sit at a table with this rabbi.

The next part of the story can be seen in two ways. All of it might take place on the road, or the next part could take place after Jesus and Zacchaeus are sitting at the table. I like the idea of it all being on the road because it's more dramatic, but regardless, what happens next is recorded for the rest of history to read, even if the crowd didn't hear the end.

When Zacchaeus agrees to host Jesus—and this would include Jesus's inner circle, too, so at least twelve more guests, if not more— the crowd grumbles.

Yes, they don't see any good that can come from this. Are they angry? Envious? Disappointed? Had Jesus let them down by not acting as they expected? This is the third year of this man's ministry, and if the gospels are telling the story right, it's rare that Jesus lived life as anyone expected.

I think they were disappointed that Zacchaeus appeared to get away with it. Jesus didn't seem to understand who this was. Possibly many of them had been victim to Zacchaeus's corruption or the corruption of other tax collectors. Didn't Jesus understand that these people on the road were victims, and Zacchaeus was a perpetrator?

I am reminded of the parable of the workers in the vineyard in Matthew 20. In that tale a landowner hires people in the morning, then later, and then even later, and at the end of the day he pays them the same amount of money. Those who worked longer were put out and thought the newcomers shouldn't get similar treatment to them. While the story isn't about Zacchaeus's situation, the landowner's final question sure fits here: *Are you envious that I am generous?*

Because yes, they were. They wanted things to make sense according to their view of the world, but Jesus saw the world through different eyes. They felt Jesus had no business altering the fabric of their society, and yet he did so time and again.

A change over dinner

Jesus knows exactly how things will play out when he offers his hand to the *wrong* people. He touches the unclean, eats with the unapproved, and draws the commoners. As always, he uses these moments to teach and train and model right behavior, because his time here is short. He has to use every second to prepare his future followers, so he packs a lot into each moment.

However, he also chooses to reach people one at a time. This moment, while it had lessons for many, was about a man in a tree.

Jesus either knew of the man's change of heart or used this call and the subsequent meal to draw that heart in, but the ultimate goal here was heart change and community restoration for Zacchaeus.

After the crowd grumbles—and I'm sure Zacchaeus heard it—we next see Zacchaeus stand up, either with the crowd or at the table after the meal ends, and make a few wild promises. He says he will give half his possessions to the poor, and then he promises reparations to those he has cheated. The amount he promises is just about the upper limit of the law's requirement for stealing livestock, so it's a lot, because livestock was important. (Exodus 22:1)

Does he mean this? Was he just talking? Anyone can make big promises.

Jesus's next words suggest Zacchaeus was serious, because Jesus accepts these words as a sign of a changed heart. He links Zacchaeus back to Abraham and says he is here to seek and save the lost. Zacchaeus is home, and Jesus makes sure everyone around them knows it. *This is one of your own,* Jesus says, *and he deserves to be treated that way. Yes, he was lost, but I am in the business of bringing the lost home, as I have just shown you.*

The crowds wanted an angry prophet. They got the Shepherd.

Seen and Invited

I think we've already shown what Jesus saw here. Zacchaeus was a Jew living without the respect of his religious community. We'll assume he was taking advantage of his fellow Jews. This man was living on the fringes, and Jesus likes to sweep the fringes for the lost.

He's also a counter to the blind man down the road. Jesus isn't here only to find the lost poor. He can come for the lost rich. The lost famous and the lost insignificant. As Jesus says in Luke 5:8, God can make children of Abraham from stones, so he can certainly choose any human he wishes and draw that person into the fold.

This story also runs counter to an event that took place not long before this with another rich man. Told in three gospels, this event involved a rich young man who wants to follow Jesus. It happens only one chapter back in Luke, but I want to snag a line from the Mark passage to demonstrate how this encounter turned out: *Jesus looked at him and loved him. "One thing you lack," he said. "Go, sell everything you have and give to the poor, and you will have treasure in heaven. Then come, follow me." At this the man's face fell. He went away sad, because he had great wealth.* Mark 10:21-22

After this the disciples and Jesus converse about the difficulty for the rich to get into the kingdom, ending with Jesus saying all things are possible for God. Move ahead one chapter, and we see this demonstrated. Jesus walks up to a rich man, changes his heart, and grants him entrance into the kingdom. Object lesson successful.

This brings us right into the invitation. Zacchaeus is invited into the open, much like our bleeding woman. This man, who lives outside his spiritual community, is forced into the center. This conversation with the rabbi on the side of the road will linger in the minds of the people, especially when Zacchaeus lives out his promise to pay people back and treat them well.

He invites the man to eat with him. This is proximity again. Zacchaeus wanted to see Jesus from the security of a tree, but Jesus had much bigger plans for the man. They needed to get acquainted. Zacchaeus needed more than a glimpse to change his heart and life.

The crowd also had an invitation. In a short span of time Jesus did two things in their city, granting healing to one person and forgiveness to another. They got more excited about the healing than the forgiveness. But Jesus invites them to broaden their definition of the Sons of Abraham. He invites them to welcome all that Jesus himself welcomes. He invites them to praise not only for the healed but the forgiven.

We have to think back to the parables of the woman who sweeps her house for the coin and the shepherd who searches for his sheep. If Jesus invites someone, I have to welcome that person. I need to celebrate.

My role and yours

This brings us to the present. Jesus changes hearts. He welcomes those who seem hopelessly far away. Zacchaeus likely sinned against his people. He could have been very greedy and corrupt. But he changed, and Jesus accepted that change, and the people needed to accept that change.

Have you found yourself on either side of this dilemma? You've changed, but your spiritual community is wary? Or perhaps someone in your midst claims to have changed, and you are the wary one, especially if you've been victim to a person's sins.

These are not easy invitations. Zacchaeus's invitation demands a change of heart and a change of behavior. It may involve a sacrifice, because Zacchaeus didn't promise a small amount of his livelihood in reparation. He was all in.

The crowd's invitation involves forgiveness and welcoming someone with open arms, which always feels like a risk. It involves leaving behind the victim attitude and celebrating with the angels that the lost are found. Oh, it's so much easier to be a victim than to take a risk.

And yet that's what Jesus asked of people in this passage. He saw Zacchaeus's heart and loved him. He saw the crowd's hearts and loved them. The Shepherd needed his sheep to get along and care for one another.

The crowd in your life might not forgive quickly or easily or at all, but that doesn't negate Jesus's love for you. And if you're in the crowd, know what Jesus expects of you. Take the risk. Open your arms to the one who feels like a bad bet.

From here we move to a story that takes place after Jesus's resurrection, one final story of Jesus restoring a lost lamb to his community. We've seen that Jesus can restore those lost through no fault of their own. We've seen he can restore those lost through sin who don't find forgiveness from their people. Now we visit Peter who, like Zacchaeus, is separated through his own actions, but unlike Zacchaeus, he has the background and relationship with Jesus to know better. This story isn't just about restoration of community but of Jesus healing a heart as a means of restoring community.

Restoration after a Fall

When I chose to include the story of Jesus reinstating Peter after his betrayal, it seemed so simple. Then I began to read what scholars and commentators had to say, and I discovered hundreds of pages and thousands of words have been spent discussing the twenty-first chapter of John. And largely, they all disagree with one another on many points.

I debated leaving it out, but I kept returning. As much as I didn't want to step into a story with so much debate, what I want to pull from it is fairly straightforward, and the main message is pertinent to all of us, because all of us have been in Peter's—and the disciples'—situation. This is a story about Jesus restoring hearts after those hearts sin and then placing his beloved, forgiven lambs back in community.

This isn't a story about Jesus meeting anyone on the road. This deals with those who have already met Jesus and accepted his call to follow. Zacchaeus is a similar story in that sin and forgiveness are involved, but he's new to faith. Peter and the disciples have to return after their faith fails them. I don't know about you, but sometimes my faith fails me and I need restored.

So let's jump in. The story has two sections. The first deals with seven disciples, and I include it because one, I love this story. It simply makes me happy. And two, it is a fascinating view of the community of the disciples. They lived with Jesus for three years, and this is a glimpse of how they handled community when he was removed from them.

We start with the disciples in Galilee. At the resurrection, an angel told Mary to have the disciples meet him in Galilee, so we'll assume that's why they're here. However, Jesus isn't immediately present, so they are waiting.

Peter is with six others, and he suggests they go fishing. This is his home, and he has a boat, and they need some income because everyone needs income, so they fish. They stay out all night without luck. Anyone who has ever fished understands that this isn't abnormal. Sometimes the fish are there, and sometimes they're not.

This is where the commentators begin to argue. Some say this group was sinning by staying busy waiting for Jesus. They should have been preaching. By fishing they were giving up on Jesus. I respectfully disagree. Jesus hasn't yet commissioned them to preach. They are still grieving, still processing this new Jesus who pops in and out, and they are waiting in Galilee hoping for answers. Nothing is the same as it was a few days ago, so they retreat to something familiar while they process.

The *IVP New Testament Commentary* has something to say about this, and I wholeheartedly agree this is vital. *More important is the simple fact that they are together. Jesus had formed the nucleus of the new community during his ministry and had further established it at the cross and in the breathing of the Spirit.*[1]

It's common in a military operation to take out the leader. If the leader is gone, most armies will fall. Jesus had been removed as leader. The Enemy seemed to have won a huge battle. And while Jesus has returned, the disciples have only seen him a time or two, and I'm going to guess they're not sure about the future of their group.

However, even without Jesus at the helm, they stick together. In the locked room before Jesus appears, they are together. Now they wait and work together. This community is solid.

It shouldn't be. At the end all of them fled. Peter betrayed Jesus outright. Human nature would have them upset with one another, throwing blame, each trying to look better than the others, perhaps not trusting one another. But no, they're fishing together.

The Shepherd shows up

Jesus arrives on the scene. Whether due to distance or supernatural intervention, the disciples on the boat don't recognize the man on the shore. The man on the shore suggests they try again with the net on the other side of the boat, and they do. Why do they trust this stranger? We don't know, except they are tired, frustrated, and already out there in the boat. What can it hurt?

The fish fill the net. One hundred fifty-three fish, possibly weighing over 300 pounds, fill the net and yet don't tear it. The haul was so large they struggled to pull it to shore.

John, or *the Disciple whom Jesus Loved*, is the first to realize Jesus's identity. He tells Peter, and Peter leaps from the boat and runs to shore. Because, whatever has gone before, Peter is still Peter, the group's zeal and charisma.

Let's back up a step. We're going to finish this section with a public restoration of Peter as a disciple. However, he is here with the disciples. They took his suggestion to fish. Peter doesn't seem to be facing censure from his friends. Peter is not on the outside of his community, at least not in the eyes of that new little community.

Also, we're not sure how Jesus and Peter are doing at this point. We know Peter wept when he betrayed Jesus. He was fully aware of his failure. However, from two passages—Luke 24:34 and 1 Corinthians 15:5—we know that Jesus had appeared to Peter early on, before he appeared to the disciples as a whole.

We can only speculate what that meeting was like. God has chosen to keep those precious moments private, only for Peter and Jesus. Did Peter weep? Did he ask forgiveness? Was he too ashamed to speak? Did he fall on his knees? Did Jesus embrace him or touch him or simply speak to him?

We don't know. But, from what we see here and the earlier group sightings of Jesus, there's reason to think Peter and Jesus are, if not reconciled, working toward it. Peter's leap from the boat suggests things are somewhat normal.

Back to our passage. John seems to have some special discernment, knowing Jesus's identity. Peter is still filled with zeal. Then the rest take the time to get the fish to shore. Jesus clearly meant for them to catch these fish, so they carefully bring them in and sort and count them.

Isn't this a great view of healthy spiritual communities? Different people with different gifts working together, all necessary to fill Jesus's purposes.

Morning on the beach

Now to my favorite part. This is one of my favorite Jesus stories in the whole Bible. He feeds them breakfast.

Yes, after being abandoned by them, dying for their sins, and coming back to life for them, he stops in to make sure they have a bite to eat after a long night.

The Shepherd is still among the sheep caring for their needs. He cannot ever do otherwise. Even as risen Lord and King, he will continue to shepherd those he loves.

This is where the commentators go a little nuts. This passage clearly reminds us of the feeding of the five thousand, except here Jesus provides the fish and bread himself. Some suggest it harks back to God feeding the Israelites in the desert. Some see symbols in the number of fish, the way Peter helps the disciples, the fact that Peter wraps in his cloak and, my personal favorite, Jesus standing peacefully on shore, almost finished with his part of the story, and the disciples fighting the nets and the lake, just beginning the challenges of their part of the story. That's a great image.

Any or all of these observations might be true, and all of them add depth to the story, but at its simplest telling, what a little child reading this story for the first time would see is that Jesus loves his disciples and feeds them breakfast.

We've seen Jesus frustrated. Exasperated. Angry. This isn't that. Jesus isn't upset with them for fishing. He's not holding a grudge against them for running away or furious with Peter for denying him.

He's feeding them. When he fed the five thousand, he did it with bowel-deep compassion. Let's assume that's the case here. He's about to leave them. Many of them are about to step into a life I do not envy. Persecution will scatter them. Some will be imprisoned. Many will experience terrible, painful deaths.

But this morning, Jesus can sit with them and relax with them and eat a meal, just like they'd done time after time during their years together. This is one of his last chances to shepherd them up close. After this, the Spirit will take that role, and while that doesn't mean Jesus isn't with us now that we have the Spirit, what he had with these men… That's about to end.

Restoration in full

But things aren't completely right. Jesus takes time at the end of the meal to speak to Peter. Since this is recorded, we assume at least one other disciple was privy to this conversation. Possibly all of them were. Jesus chooses this moment, with those disciples closest to Peter, to make sure Peter realizes his role as part of the group.

The implication is that perhaps what's keeping Peter from fully being part of this community is Peter himself. When we sin and fall, sometimes community welcomes us back. Jesus always welcomes us back. But it might take an extra moment for us to let go of our sin and take back our roles.

This passage is well known. Jesus asks Peter three times if he loves him. Peter responds yes every time. By the third time, Peter is hurt, but he again insists that he loves Jesus.

Oh, my. This is another spot where commentators have a whole lot to say, and I'm going to take a somewhat cowardly approach and slide over most of it, because I think the point is clear. However, we need to back up and break it down some, because it gives us an idea of where Peter is spiritually and where Jesus needs him to be.

The big conversation surrounding this passage is that Jesus asks Peter if he loves him using the Greek *agapeo*, which is a deep, unconditional form of love often used to describe God's love for his people. And Peter always responds using the word *phileo*, an affectionate, brotherly love. For the third asking, Jesus switches to *phileo* himself. Peter continues to answer using *phileo*.

More and more scholars are suggesting John uses the two terms interchangeably in the book of John, so there's no deeper meaning here. But many more find very deep meaning here, all kinds of meanings, many painting Peter in a very bad light.

Restoration After a Fall

But at its heart, Jesus asks Peter if he loves him, and Peter says yes. Actually, regardless of the nuances of the word love, that's exactly what happens here. And everyone agrees Jesus asks three times because Peter denied him three times. Each question heals one of those betrayal wounds.

Part of me itches to get into the nitty gritty of this, but it's not that important for this conversation. What might be important is the first time Jesus asks. Jesus says "Simon, son of John, do you love me more than these?" And two things stand out. First, Jesus isn't using the name Peter, which he gave Simon after calling him. Instead, he's returning to his pre-disciple name. This had to hurt. Second, he asks Peter to compare his love. We're not sure what the *these* are. It could be a question of Peter loving Jesus more deeply than the other disciples do, or loving Jesus more than he loved the disciples, or loving Jesus more than he loves fish and boats.

Since one of Peter's last statements before Jesus's death was a bombastic announcement that he loved Jesus enough to die for him, let's go with the first. And Peter doesn't rise to the bait. Some suggest Peter's simple *You know that I love you* is a newfound humility. Peter has failed Jesus before. Jesus knows the depth of Peter's love, but Peter isn't one hundred percent sure he won't fail again. He has faced his weakness and frailty and is more cautious now.

To me, that fits. But Jesus takes the answer as a simple yes and gives Peter a command. Each time he gives a similar command. *Feed my lambs. Take care of my sheep. Feed my sheep.*

This is huge. We know what the flock means to Jesus. He's giving Peter an enormous command and saying, in essence, *Yes, I do know how much you love me, and that's why I'm entrusting my most precious possessions to you.*

This call doesn't come without a downside. Jesus follows this up by warning Peter that hard things are coming. Peter had once said he would die for Jesus. (Actually, this is after Jesus talks about dying for a friend—a philos. So maybe when Peter says he loves Jesus using *phileo*, that's what he's thinking. He loves Jesus like a friend, a friend he'd die for.) Now Jesus suggests he's going to get a chance to prove that.

Maybe the question to Peter was never *Do you love me?* but *How much do you love me?* And Peter, answering with the love of a friend, is answering that he loves him as much as a person can love, a love that will lay down its life for the other. This time, that will prove to be true.

A powerful future

This passage ends with the reinstatement. Three years earlier, Jesus asked Peter to follow him from the shore of this lake. Now he does it again. He very clearly says *Follow Me*. Whatever the disciples or Peter may think about Peter as a disciple, it's now fully clear. Peter is one of them again, no questions asked.

And, while we don't hear Peter's answer here, nor do we hear Jesus call Peter by the name Peter, the writer of this gospel never stops calling Simon by the name Peter. Most commentators agree this section was written after Peter's death, so in calling the man Peter, the writer lets us know that Peter was a fully called and realized disciple to the very end.

We also see this in Peter's own words. Peter pens two letters in the Bible. In them he calls himself Peter. He calls himself a servant and an apostle. The books are rich and show a mature, humble man who learned from his failure and accepted Jesus's call to shepherd the sheep. Here are a couple verses that speak of this forgiven, restored Peter's view on things:

Finally, all of you, be like-minded, be sympathetic, love one another, be compassionate and humble. 1 Peter 3:8

And he speaks to the elders of the church, giving them a call similar to what was given to him: *Be shepherds of God's flock that is under your care, watching over them—not because you must, but because you are willing, as God wants you to be; not pursuing dishonest gain, but eager to serve; [3] not lording it over those entrusted to you, but being examples to the flock.* 1 Peter 5:2-3

Seen and Invited

Jesus finds his disciples fishing one morning. They're not catching anything, but they are working together. They seem to have forgiven one another. He helps them in their work, feeds them, and then restores one who might not be accepting Jesus's forgiveness.

What did Jesus see? We mentioned it, but let's just say it again. He saw his sheep. He saw some of his most beloved, precious sheep. He saw their years of learning and effort, the failures of their pasts, and a remarkable and yet bleak future for many of them. His heart went out to them, and he spent time with them before everything changed.

He saw Peter's new humility. He's still Peter, leaping from the boat in his zeal to get to Jesus, because proximity matters even to the humble. He saw John, who would one day give witness to the end of the age, discern Jesus's identity before anyone else. He saw the rest of the men simply carrying on with the fish Jesus had given them. We don't even get names for each of them, but they did their jobs and were fed a meal in Jesus's presence just like the rest. All were necessary and vital to the story, just as a community should be.

And the invitation? *Throw out your net.* They had no idea why Jesus told them to put their net out again after a fruitless night, but taking that suggestion gave them a heap of fish. Yes, this has deeper meaning, because we all think straight back to Jesus's promise to his disciples that fishing for fish will become fishing for men, and all of us following Jesus are on a road of discipleship.

Bring some of your fish. Again, we do what we do and lay the results at Jesus's feet. Peter went straight back into the water to help the rest bring the fish to shore. He didn't want to miss out on anything Jesus told him to do.

Then *Come and have breakfast.* They had questions. It says they knew who he was, but they didn't ask anything. Instead, they ate. They enjoyed the company of their beloved but now changed rabbi. They let Jesus break bread over them and feed them.

Then Peter is invited to shepherd. *Feed my lambs. Take care of my sheep.* But Peter doesn't see that as a call to himself alone, because he passes that call forward to the elders in the new churches.

And finally, to Peter he says, for the second time, *Follow me.* Peter accepts this call, and this time, in the face of the worst hardship, he follows to the end. This invitation to come to Jesus isn't limited to the twelve disciples. One of the very final calls of the Bible, in Revelation 22, is from the Spirit and it's a call to everyone reading the book: *Come.* Rev. 22:17

Comfort in community

What do we do with this story? A pastor friend of mine is fond of saying that the days from Easter to Jesus's ascension were all about him healing the blown-out hearts of his disciples. Jesus arrived on the beach to comfort. He offered physical comfort in a financially valuable catch of fish and a meal. He offered the emotional comfort of his company, stepping back into his place in their little community for nearly the last time. He offered spiritual comfort in restoring and clarifying for all of them their gifts and callings. He would later see all of them and give more words of mission, but this was a start. This was the low-key version. Perhaps these seven were the most broken after their abandonment of Jesus. Or perhaps Jesus simply used the moment on the beach to reenact his earlier visit to the beach when several of these men answered their first call.

I will fail. I will sin. Jesus will continue to be the shepherd who seeks the lost sheep and restores each of us wanderers back to the fold. When I shock myself with the depths of my sin and failure, when I betray my own heart while betraying my Shepherd, he will hear my cry for forgiveness, and he will come and minister. He still invites those he loves to eat on the beach. As Elijah was fed by an angel before being sent on mission, Jesus feeds his children before they step out into their missions, too.

Each of us has our own version of the mission. I might need to jump out of the boat. I might be given the discernment to see Jesus working and light a fire under the Peters around me. I might be asked to stay in the boat and fight with the net.

But whatever I'm asked to do, it's within a community.

Community is messy and difficult, so Jesus spent three years modeling how it should work, and here we see it working. In the face of uncertainty, these men stayed together. They were going to process the strange twists in their story together.

In the book of Acts, persecution scatters many of these men, along with the other disciples outside the twelve. But the community started here would keep them in contact. From this community came accountability, the means to quench many heretical ideas, and the beginnings of the formal church that would linger through this very moment.

Community is vital to Jesus, so he worked hard to restore those on the roads to their families and their people, for their protection, their growth, and for the protection and growth of the entire kingdom.

Many things can keep us out of community with our spiritual family. Whatever your reason, Jesus shows that he longs for you to belong. He takes pains to draw his loved ones together, tells us to be united, and shows us how to do it by allying with twelve very human men for three years, working with their fears, their weaknesses, and their temperaments.

Know that, regardless of how your human community is doing, Jesus considers you fully in communion with him. You are accepted, and nothing keeps him from coming in to dine with you. Not your past, not how others see you, not your fears and hesitation, and not your sinful moments. Jesus sees you and still wants you to be part of his glorious kingdom.

As you get to know Jesus's great desire to dine with you, reach out to others drifting down isolation road. Collect your tribe and walk together. Draw others close. But whatever you do, don't settle for life alone. The road of isolation is a dangerous place where it's easy to hear lies and to be picked off by the hardships of the world. Your community is your safety net. Find them, love them, and accept their imperfections as they accept yours while we journey further down the road.

Section Five: The Flat Road of Insignificance

This is where it all comes together. We've battled brokenness, faced doubts, been fulfilled, and planted our roots in community. The final road of our journey is the most important one, as we trade the empty, flat, pointless road of insignificance for the vivid, ever-changing landscape surrounding the road of purpose.

You and I are his for a reason. God has purposes for each person rescued on the roads. (Eph. 2:10) You have tasks set up just for you. Meanwhile, I'll undertake tasks just for me, and together we'll build a kingdom where we can be seen and known and loved for eternity.

We've seen some of this already, because of course Jesus doesn't break his encounters into single purposes. Many left the feet of Jesus and went on to new things. The blind began life with sight. Those separated from their community left Jesus and belonged. The frightened left Jesus with the courage to do life with new vigor.

But a few moments on the road are very universal, and I chose three stories here to demonstrate one broad purpose all of us embrace.

In a world of flashing screens and digital identities and the constant search for something new, having a solid purpose that lasts through the end—this gives life texture and color and ties everything together.

We weren't meant to wander aimlessly, so let's hike down this final road, the flat, boring, colorless road of insignificance, and help a few souls over to the vibrant, robust, sometimes dangerous but always rewarding road of purpose.

Come and See

Maybe *THE* universal purpose of the Christian is to be a disciple and make disciples. I will be very honest. I wanted to skip some of this. When I think of making disciples, I imagine accosting strangers and convincing them to follow Jesus. My introvert self shudders. The idea of fishing for men isn't a purpose I embrace with open arms.

However, the passages we're about to look at make it clear that's not the meat of our discipleship. It's time to get a clearer view of being a disciple and making disciples. One of Jesus's final commands to his disciples was to make more disciples, so this command has weight. Let's try to figure it out and do it well.

I think, once we see it clearly, it's a practice—a lifestyle—even the biggest introvert and most timid soul will adopt with zeal.

We're looking at two main passages, and at first they don't seem to fit together. I'm going to assume anyone reading this wants to get closer to Jesus, and that means something might have kept you away. One of the things that trips up new—or old—Christians is seeming contradictions in the Bible, so let's clear up one of those.

Let's start with Mark 1:16-17, which reads like this: *As Jesus walked beside the Sea of Galilee, he saw Simon and his brother Andrew casting a net into the lake, for they were fishermen.* [17] *"Come, follow me," Jesus said, "and I will send you out to fish for people."* [18] *At once they left their nets and followed him.*

This is rough, and honestly it doesn't sound like the Jesus we see in most of the Gospels. He shows up to strangers, crooks his finger, and they follow like zombies, leaving their lives behind?

No. Of course not. Ancient Middle Eastern storytelling was a little different from our own. For instance, the writers didn't always follow a clear chronology. Like I've done here, they lumped some events together to follow a theme.

Two other things they do is compress a story, which we've also seen, and compress time. Mark's telling moves fast. *And then, and then, and then...* Three years shoot past. But we know more happened. Three years takes three years to live. But his writing style was to point out what he considered the highlights along the way.

Compressing a story is the same. Each writer wrote from a different perspective and pointed out different details. Same stories, different telling.

Does that make them false? No. It just means the point of the Gospels isn't straight history. It's meant to tell us everything we need to know to identify and love Jesus.

However, it also has to make sense, because it's about real, historical moments. So, what took place that led to the disciples being called? Did Jesus speak a single phrase and call them? Or, as we'll see in Luke, did he hop randomly into a fisherman's boat and then call him? Why don't the tales seem to line up?

John tells Andrew...

The key to these stories lies in the *Gospel of John*. Commentators agree John wrote his book last. I find myself wondering if he didn't use his tale to fill in some gaps that the previous books didn't share, to add texture and explanation. The further people got from Jesus's life—and the further they were from geographical Israel, the more they might need some things explained.

So, we're going to start here in John 1, which takes us back before the Mark boat incident. Verses 35-40 read like this:

35 The next day John was there again with two of his disciples. 36 When he saw Jesus passing by, he said, "Look, the Lamb of God!"

37 When the two disciples heard him say this, they followed Jesus. 38 Turning around, Jesus saw them following and asked, "What do you want?"

They said, "Rabbi" (which means "Teacher"), "where are you staying?"

39 "Come," he replied, "and you will see."

So they went and saw where he was staying, and they spent that day with him. It was about four in the afternoon.

Verse 40 tells us this was Andrew and an unnamed man, possibly John, and they were already disciples of John the Baptist. This pair was already living with a disciple mindset. John the Baptist calls Jesus *the Lamb of God*, and the pair, interests piqued, follows him on the shore out of curiosity.

Jesus, ever the gentle Shepherd, sees them and asks what they want. The gospel writer never says Jesus was preaching. He wasn't doing miracles. This is my starting point for writing this entire book, the moment when two men turn to Jesus on a simple recommendation and end up following him. What did they see? What happened that day?

They tell him they want to spend the day with him. No, not directly, because this is ancient Israel, and protocol says you don't invite yourself for dinner. But that's what they wanted. They wanted to know Jesus more, to see why John had called him the Lamb of God. They wanted to be with him.

Because, as I have said more than once, proximity matters when it comes to Jesus.

We don't know where he was staying. We can assume from the timeline that these men likely spent the night. This is another private, personal conversation, much like Jesus's first post-resurrection conversation with Peter. Jesus has personal relationships with each of his lambs, and what happened that day was theirs.

Who tells Simon...

Either on the way to spend the day with Jesus or right after this, Andrew goes for his brother Simon. This would be the first time Simon and Jesus meet, and Jesus looks at Simon in verse 42 and gives him a new name.

At this point we don't know anything about Simon's personality or his future, but Jesus does. He calls him *Cephas* (Aramaic), which is *Petros* in Greek, from which we get his commonly known name Peter. It means rock.

This has to be huge for Peter. Abram was renamed. Jacob, too. Simon would see the significance of this. A rabbi his brother trusts, one that John the Baptist trusts, has just given him a new name, and that means something significant is in his future.

From what we know about Peter, doesn't this make sense? Peter was a doer, a guy who would look for significance and purpose. To him, being renamed would have great meaning. Jesus let Andrew and his friend come and stay and see, which was what they wanted, what they needed to draw close to Jesus. Then Jesus gives Peter a new name and a new purpose, exactly what he needed to draw close to Jesus.

This is a pattern we've seen all along, Jesus calling each of his lambs in a unique way tailored to individual needs and personalities.

We see no long-term call here. Discipleship didn't always mean spending full time with someone. Some disciples—and some rabbis—had jobs.[1] Paul, on his missions, continued as a tentmaker. So, Jesus first approached these men before John the Baptist was imprisoned, but he hadn't yet become a full-time wandering rabbi with full-time disciples. That happens after John's execution, perhaps as much as a year later.

Then comes Philip…

Next we have Philip. We get very little on this call. We know Andrew, Philip, and Peter are from the same town of Bethsaida (John 1:44). Perhaps Philip already knew Jesus. Perhaps Philip only knew of Jesus. But in this case, Jesus approaches and makes his call. *Follow me*, he says. (John 1:43) It's simple, and John gives us nothing more about it. However, what Philip does with this call, his immediate next step, tells us a little bit about him. Like Andrew, Philip wants to share what he's learned with someone special to him.

Who goes for Nathanael

So Philip, after his call, finds another friend and shares his news. This is starting to sound like a game of telephone, where the message is passed down the line. With great excitement, these men, possibly all interrelated, possibly not, discover Jesus and begin to bring their friends and loved ones to see.

Philip's friend Nathanael brings us to an interesting story. I'm going to tell it, because it says a lot about how we make disciples. It's also a story the wordsmith/historian in me cannot ignore.

The story goes like this:

45 Philip found Nathanael and told him, "We have found the one Moses wrote about in the Law, and about whom the prophets also wrote—Jesus of Nazareth, the son of Joseph."
46 "Nazareth! Can anything good come from there?" Nathanael asked.
"Come and see," said Philip.
47 When Jesus saw Nathanael approaching, he said of him, "Here truly is an Israelite in whom there is no deceit."
48 "How do you know me?" Nathanael asked.
Jesus answered, "I saw you while you were still under the fig tree before Philip called you."
49 Then Nathanael declared, "Rabbi, you are the Son of God; you are the king of Israel."
50 Jesus said, "You believe because I told you I saw you under the fig tree. You will see greater things than that." 51 He then added, "Very truly I tell you, you will see 'heaven open, and the angels of God ascending and descending on the Son of Man." John 1:45-51

Philip suggests Jesus might be the Messiah, and Nathanael doubts. The Messiah isn't supposed to come from Nazareth. There has to be a mistake. Nathanael doesn't think Philip is right. Instead of arguing, Philip simply says come and see for yourself.

Yes, he lets Jesus do the convincing.

When Nathanael arrives, Jesus calls him an Israelite in whom is no deceit.

Nathanael asks Jesus how he knows him, and Jesus says he saw him under the fig tree before Philip called him. This is a sycamore fig, the kind Zacchaeus hid in. It had big leaves and lots of shade. When Nathanael hears this, he believes Jesus is the Son of God—likely meaning a prophet. Jesus then tells Nathanael he will see greater things than a simple knowledge of a man under a tree, that he will see *heaven open, and the angels of God ascending and descending on the Son of Man,* a quote from Genesis. (28:12)

A little verbal play

We could fall into a deep rabbit hole here, and I don't want to do that. However, we're going to skirt the rim, because this is a beautiful scene. Jesus's humor shows up here, his gentle way of reaching individual souls. I simply cannot walk away from all the nuances of this conversation.

Perhaps this happened exactly as we read it. Nathanael trusts Jesus because Jesus supernaturally saw him under a tree. However, *under the fig tree* was also a rabbinical saying at the time to describe meditation on the law, which often happened under a tree to utilize the shade.[2] So Jesus could mean both, or he could simply be saying he knew Nathanael was studying the law when Philip found him.

Here's where it gets fun. Look at how Philip introduced Nathanael to the idea of Jesus. He mentions Moses and the prophets. Philip knew Nathanael cared about the law, and so he used that to draw him. Jesus does them same, only he does it even better.

Fully three times Jesus makes an allusion to the patriarch Jacob, and it has to be said with an air of humor. Jesus begins this conversation speaking of *Israel*—the patriarch Jacob's new name—and *deceit*—the meaning of Jacob's original name. We can assume, if Nathanael was studying the Scripture when Philip found him, he was reading this passage in Genesis.

Nathanael was startled because Jesus knew exactly what he had been reading. Perhaps this went even deeper to what Nathanael had been thinking about the passage. This stranger shares an inside joke of sorts with Nathanael based on his current Bible study.

Then Jesus quotes from Jacob's dealings with God again. The Genesis passage Jesus alludes to speaks of Jacob dreaming about angels ascending and descending to heaven.

So maybe what Jesus says to Nathanael is *I know you study the law. In fact, you were just studying Jacob. I know the truths matter to you. You are earnest in your zeal for my father's words, and I am here to fulfill them.*

That dream about the angels — I can do more, and you can be involved.

No surprise, Nathanael, who apparently loves the law and the history, is hooked.

Wooed, not called

What we get from this passage in John is that the disciples weren't called with a crooked finger and a single word. Jesus wooed them. He met each man where he was.

He also didn't lead them out immediately. They had time. Yes, they might have joined Jesus for a while, but if our understanding of the timeline is right—and it might not be—Jesus doesn't name his twelve men for some time yet. The disciples seem to come and go in the stories for a while. John still has to be imprisoned. For these days, however many they are, these men will have time to hear Jesus, visit a time or two, and ponder. Then their beloved John, the rabbi more than one of them followed, is taken from them.

After this, we move to the passages in Matthew, Mark, and Luke. Not until then do these men become full-time disciples of Jesus and leave their boats.

But let's not go there yet. I'm not ready to leave these men. This passage started this whole book, and I want to go back to the question that started it and make sure we understand what happened here before we get to the next part, where these men do leave their lives to follow Jesus full time.

Back in Epiphany of 2023, my pastor spoke on this passage and asked why the men wanted to spend time with Jesus. Why did they want to follow? We don't know if Jesus was already preaching. If so, his words might have played a role. We are pretty sure he wasn't performing miracles yet, as we are told his first public miracle happened later in Cana once he had at least a few part-time disciples.

But all of these men spent time with Jesus and started collecting friends to do the same. They wanted to be part of this movement which wasn't a movement yet. They saw a future here that they wanted to be part of.

It starts with a simple question Jesus asks two disciples: *What do you want?* (1:38), to which they answer with a question, because they were too polite to come out and say what they wanted.

Rabbi, where are you staying?

Then he seals the deal with this answer, this promise, these words that will take on so much more meaning as time passes.

Come, and you will see.

From here in the future we can't help but hear other, similar words echo through time.

Come and see what God has done... Ps. 66:5

Come, you who are weary... Matt. 11:28

Come...(out of the boat into the water)Matt.14:29

Let the little children come... Matt.19:16

Let anyone who is thirsty come to me... John 7:27

And when Nathanael doubts, Philip says *Come and see*.

The men Jesus calls in this passage were looking for God. They were studying the law, following the most recent prophet, searching for meaning. Jesus sees each of them. He approaches each differently, knowing exactly how to reach each man, each heart.

Then he simply extends an invitation. And it's a simple one. Come. See. It's not a command to stay, but to try. *Let me convince you,* he says. *Give me a shot.*

They do. Later, when he calls them to full-time discipleship, they are ready to go.

What about us?

So what does this mean for you and me and our purpose? Well, each of these men, regardless of how they got there, was invited by Jesus himself. Jesus's own words and actions drew them.

So how do disciples happen today? This is pretty cool, because the answer is in Matthew 28:18-20: *All authority in heaven and on earth has been given to me. Therefore go and make disciples... teaching them to obey...*

Jesus calls his disciples. Every person who accepts the call to discipleship hears from Jesus's Spirit in his heart. But you and I are given the authority to make the introductions. We are to speak his words, be his voice, and make the invitation for others to come and see.

Now we're back to that scary thought of evangelizing the stranger at the mall. That's not what we see. We see the call as a wooing. Jesus called people where he was. He will bring those we are to woo into our orbits.

Sure, sometimes he moves a person's orbit. A dear family I know moved to Egypt a few years ago to be full-time missionaries. However, I know enough of their process to know they still draw people within their orbits. They are simply intentional about where those orbits lie. They make relationships, serve, and honor the people around them, just like Jesus did.

As Jesus found men thirsty for purpose on the road and used many methods to call them, so do we. We give names to those who need new names. We speak of things that interest those we woo, like Jesus did with Nathanael. Sometimes we call out to someone, and sometime we live our lives and someone comes with questions.

The comfort of limits

What we can't do is change a heart. Philip simply asked Nathanael to come and see. Jesus said the same to John's disciples.

Isn't that easier than feeling like the fate of everyone in my orbit is on my shoulders? I represent Jesus well by knowing him through the Scripture and the Spirit. And I then I introduce him and extend an invitation to give this a try. *Come and see.*

Taste and see, David suggests in Psalm 34. *Taste and see that the Lord is good; blessed is the one who takes refuge in him.* Psalm 34:8

So I tell those around me how to taste. I let them know how to take refuge. Then Jesus and the Spirit take it from there.

I mentioned what Jesus saw here, but let's make it more official. In Andrew and the unnamed man, he saw men who already wished to learn from men of God. He saw men who wanted to know more, men who thought spending time with this unknown Jesus would answer their questions. He saw men seeking God with their whole lives.

In Peter he saw a man whose name couldn't contain him, a man who needed a formal outward change to match the inward change that would happen. He saw a man who trusted his brother the same way the brother trusted John the Baptist, again a man seeking God.

He saw Philip, whose first thought after being called by Jesus was to get his friend. Philip wanted to share the good news with someone he loved, and yet when that person doubted, he simply held out his hand and offered an invitation.

And when Jesus saw Nathanael, he saw a man already devoted to the Words of God, a man who would understand so much of what Jesus was about to do, a man who would catch Jesus's allusions and Biblical imagery. I wonder if he ever pointed them out to the other disciples. They started their relationship with a little verbal sparring and teasing, and I suspect that never stopped.

And of course, we discussed the invitation to come and see. What I didn't mention was that, at its most basic, this would be an invitation to live life together. Andrew and his friend spent the night with Jesus right off. Hospitality and proximity are vital in discipleship.

Jesus called men not just to learn from him. He didn't call them just to trust in him or believe in him. This wasn't an ego trip to accumulate as much power and popularity as possible.

He also didn't collect men to believe and then leave them behind, moving on to find others to believe. It went much deeper.

He invited them to live life with him. And that's the next part of our purpose. Let me boldly posit that it's the more important part of our purpose. Sure, we find the lost and offer them a chance to come, and that can happen in as many ways as there are people. But then we walk the road together.

Live with your eyes open. Where are people you can speak to? If you speak science, find the science people. If you speak healing, find the broken. If you speak to children, find children. Jesus knew how to speak to everyone in all their heart languages, but you and I will have a smaller audience. So find it.

And then read on as Jesus demonstrates that fishing for men doesn't mean dumping them in a net and moving on. We catch them alive, and while we all swim in our aquariums together (Excuse my strange analogy, but maybe the man who called fishermen would appreciate it…) we live our lives together.

Because this road of purpose hinges not just on us calling disciples, but being disciples and training disciples. It's as varied and textured and rich as the people who walk it.

And walking this road is the most rewarding, difficult, wonderful thing we can be called to do.

Gone Fishin'

John sets the discipleship stage by showing us the first calling of the disciples, only it's a general call. Commentators seem to agree this isn't where the men come to him full time. However, it assures us some of them knew Jesus and his ministry from the beginning.

Peter is one of those, and Luke gives us an extended passage to explain Peter's call to full-time discipleship. I want to hang out there for a little while.

Matthew and Mark give us two short paragraphs about this. I think these little paragraphs are misunderstood and give the wrong impression of how Jesus called, which we talked about before. So we looked to John for the back story, and now Luke illuminates the Matthew and Mark story.

Here's how Mark tells the story of the call of Peter, James, and John:

As Jesus walked beside the Sea of Galilee, he saw Simon and his brother Andrew casting a net into the lake, for they were fishermen. [17] *"Come, follow me," Jesus said, "and I will send you out to fish for people."* [18] *At once they left their nets and followed him.*
[19] *When he had gone a little farther, he saw James son of Zebedee and his brother John in a boat, preparing their nets.* [20] *Without delay he called them, and they left their father Zebedee in the boat with the hired men and followed him.* Mark 1:16-20

We mentioned this in the last chapter and how it isn't as straightforward as it seems. Mark is leaving a lot out of the narrative. It seems his point is that the disciples were called by God, they had a specific purpose in being called, and they had to sacrifice to take the call. All true.

Luke gives us more, and where John shows us Jesus's various methods of calling his people, Luke gives us more hints as to our purpose as disciples. Remember, the disciples were told at the end to make disciples all over the earth. If you trust Jesus, you are the recipient of that command. You are to be a disciple, learning more about Jesus and living for him, and you are meant to make disciples, both calling and training them. We talked a little bit about calling disciples. Let's talk more about being a disciple and how to disciple others, essentially taking the role of rabbi. First, let's hear what Luke has to say:

One day as Jesus was standing by the Lake of Gennesaret, the people were crowding around him and listening to the word of God. ² He saw at the water's edge two boats, left there by the fishermen, who were washing their nets. ³ He got into one of the boats, the one belonging to Simon, and asked him to put out a little from shore. Then he sat down and taught the people from the boat.
⁴ *When he had finished speaking, he said to Simon, "Put out into deep water, and let down the nets for a catch."*
⁵ *Simon answered, "Master, we've worked hard all night and haven't caught anything. But because you say so, I will let down the nets."*
⁶ *When they had done so, they caught such a large number of fish that their nets began to break. ⁷ So they signaled their partners in the other boat to come and help them, and they came and filled both boats so full that they began to sink.*
⁸ *When Simon Peter saw this, he fell at Jesus' knees and said, "Go away from me, Lord; I am a sinful man!" ⁹ For he and all his companions were astonished at the catch of fish they had taken, ¹⁰ and so were James and John, the sons of Zebedee, Simon's partners.*
Then Jesus said to Simon, "Don't be afraid; from now on you will fish for people." ¹¹ So they pulled their boats up on shore, left everything and followed him. Luke 5:1-11

Luke 5:1-11 most likely takes place within the Mark passage. Jesus sees his fishermen friends at the lake. They are cleaning nets and/or doing a little fishing from the shore. Since they are not actively fishing from the boats, Jesus asks for their help, because he has a crowd here, and he needs to be heard.

This sounds familiar. Remember when Jesus spoke with the woman at the well? He asked for her help. He does the same with Peter. Being a disciple means our lives intertwine with others. Jesus had an honest problem here, a crowd that jostled and struggled to hear. Peter had a boat, and the shoreline created an amphitheater effect to direct sound.

Jesus knew Peter—he'd renamed him, spent time at his home, and healed his mother-in-law just a chapter before this (Luke 4:38-39). Peter easily agrees to help the rabbi. While Jesus speaks, Peter and his men would have kept the boat still, holding against the current.[1] We don't know who else was in the boat, although we can assume Andrew was one from our *Mark* passage, but it sounds like there were more than these two.

Listening to the rabbi and holding the boat for him was likely more fun than cleaning nets and doing the chores of a fisherman.

When Jesus finishes with the crowd, he suggests that Peter take the boat deeper and let down the nets.

Because you say so...

Peter follows this with the beginning of an argument. He points out they fished all night—the time when fish actually schooled in this sea—and had failed, so clearly this area isn't swimming in fish. Also, it's daytime. Fish are caught at night. But he then corrects himself, maybe as he remembers his mother-in-law's healing, or as he realizes he's arguing with the rabbi. I imagine him making his excuse and then smiling as he adds *If you say so*. He already knows enough about Jesus to know this man can surprise him.

What happens next? They catch so many fish their nets begin to break, and they signal their partners for help.

Author Kenneth Bailey points out an interesting but somewhat irrelevant thought about them signaling their partners instead of calling to them.[2] They had this amazing catch, and all night they—and maybe their fellow fishermen—had come up empty. Instead of calling everyone to let them know where to find a big haul, they signal. Bailey calls this ancient Middle Eastern cunning, keeping details of their business to themselves. This may not be relevant to anything we're discussing, but it sure paints these men in a more human light, doesn't it?

Commentary writer Craig Keener points out that fishermen made a better-than-average living.[3] Purchasing a boat, especially one large enough for multiple fishermen, isn't cheap. Then add to that these boats worked in a partnership, and we have some savvy men on the water with Jesus. He tells these savvy fishermen how to do their business, and they do it.

And they get the big haul. This will more than make up for their long, wasted night.

Peter's response goes like this: *When Simon Peter saw this, he fell at Jesus' knees and said, "Go away from me, Lord; I am a sinful man!" For he and all his companions were astonished at the catch of fish they had taken, and so were James and John, the sons of Zebedee, Simon's partners.* (Luke 5:8-10).

The IVP commentary has this to say about this passage: *The greatest moment in their fishing career causes them to stop and ponder what God is doing. Jesus has taken Peter's humble faith and scared him to death with God's presence.*[4]

Peter has seen Jesus heal. But as we found with the walking on water passage, every time Jesus does some new amazing thing, it fills his followers with new wonder.

Jesus jumps in here with two important things to say: *Don't be afraid;* and *from now on you will fish for people.* Luke 5:10b

First, Jesus's intention wasn't to instill fear, so he stops that right away. Chronologically this may be one of the first times he's said this to a potential follower, but it won't be the last.

Then he gives Peter a new mission. He's already been given a new name. Now he has a new mission, fishing for men. More accurately, this passage uses a word that means to catch, to catch alive, or to capture. He's using a play on the fisherman's catch but making it better. Now they are all about life.

After this, the men follow. In Mark we learned that the Zebedee brothers left their boat with their dad and the hired workers first, didn't simply abandon it on the shore, but the result was a big change.

Was it an immediate change? Did they walk away that moment? It's hard to say. Zebedee could easily have dealt with both boats, since all these men worked together. So perhaps that day they became full-time disciples. But we know these writers condense things, so we can't be sure. We see them all fishing again in the future, so it seems their business remained, and at least on occasion they returned to it.

The humanity of discipleship

So how does any of this relate to being a disciple or training disciples?

I want to go back to the beginning where Jesus asked for help. Jesus never had to ask anyone for help. He had the ability to move as he wished within this world. Seas and fig trees and demons and illnesses listened to him. Yet he chose to ask for help sometimes.

Maybe he does this because all of us eventually take his teaching role, and we *do* have to ask for help. A body of believers usually has many people at different stages along the way, and we reach back and help those behind us to catch up. At some level, we play rabbi with one another.

The rabbi entwined his life with his disciples. Their relationship was one of give and take. As humans, no teacher has all the answers, nor do students have nothing to offer. Discipleship isn't a classroom. It's a life course.

Ann Spangler, in her book on Jesus as a rabbi, says *This made sense in light of the fact that the goal wasn't academic learning but personal transformation.*[5]

This explains Jesus's exasperation at times. This wasn't a course of memorization and quizzes. This was about their lives. Personally he wanted them to grow. Then they had to pass these lessons forward, because each generation learns from the one behind. We have the Word and the Spirit to keep us on track, but humans play a huge role. We learn to live a godly life by seeing them lived around us and by participating in them being lived around us.

We are all on this road together, even Jesus. And while he had nothing to learn, he fully participated in humanity with us. He lived transparently, as we saw when he called them friends and promised to share with them. And sometimes he let them help him.

Authority and Provision

Next we see Jesus provide. After a fruitless night of fishing, Jesus gave the word, and the boat was swamped with fish. After this, these men followed Jesus full time. Their businesses would suffer. We know Peter had a wife, and he might not have been the only one. They had to know Jesus would provide.

And he did. Big, wild provision. Asking men to follow part time didn't require a miracle. But this next stage does. Jesus never asked them to turn their backs on those counting on them. Instead, he assures them that with him provision will happen.

When Peter is faced with Jesus's authority over fish—an area where Peter likely felt like he had the upper hand—he falls at Jesus's knees. He puts himself in that submissive position we've seen so many times. Peter fell to that place and called for mercy. The words loosely come from Isaiah, who finds himself in the throne room of heaven and calls out in fear, thinking he cannot be there and live to tell the tale. The holiness of God screams to us our own unholiness.

Peter felt that fear when he realized the scope of Jesus's authority. Jesus was suddenly much too big. He was no longer a wandering rabbi. He wasn't even on par with most prophets. He was bigger, and in Peter's lifetime—and several generations before that—God hadn't moved like this in Israel.

Something big was happening, and Peter didn't know if he was qualified to participate.

As a disciple, I understand that. Jesus is building a kingdom, and it has some great enemies. Am I enough to stand in the fray? Can I be here with Jesus and the Spirit changing the world? It feels much too big.

And yet Jesus says I must. That was Jesus's call. Don't just be a disciple, learning from and emulating Jesus, but be a rabbi. Be a shepherd.

That's when Jesus says not to be afraid. He tells them from now on they will catch men alive. Take captives. We're stealing people from the enemy. We're giving life to the walking dead. Is it a big job? Yes. Am I enough? No. That's okay, because the Spirit is here to do the heavy lifting.

Like Philip brought Nathaniel and let Jesus explain himself, I can bring people to Jesus and let him explain himself, too, through the Spirit who speaks to their spirits through the Bible, through the teaching of spiritual leaders, and through my life as I participate, whether it's preaching on the road or making dinner for my family.

Seen and Invited

What did Jesus see that day? A lot happened on the shore that afternoon. Jesus saw a crowd that needed to give him their attention and hear his words. He needed to step back so they would see him, and Peter and his fishing partners made that happen.

He saw men who had started to know him, men who followed John, who cared about their mothers-in-law, who wanted new names and purposes. These men were searching for spiritual answers and spiritual truths. They were willing to listen and learn, even taking fishing advice from a carpenter-turned-rabbi who shouldn't have known the first thing about fishing.

They had a fair amount of wealth. Peter often hosted in his home, and he and a group of men had large boats and hired help. Were they rich like tax collectors? Probably not. But they were doing well. They had areas of expertise and the respect of employees.

Jesus then saw the people who needed to be caught alive. Not just that moment, but down through the ages. When he spoke of those future people, that's you and me. We were there in that story. Jesus worked hard to train these men for you and for me. And he wants us to work and train hard for those after us. All of us rely on those before us, and those after us rely on us.

So what was the invitation for these men?

Follow me, he said. He doesn't say it in the Luke passage, but he does in Matthew and Mark. *Follow me.*

Change directions. Pull the boat to the edge and walk a new road. Don't worry about the boat—I've got that. Don't worry about the food. I've got that, too. I have seen you. I have named you, called you, and shown you my authority. I've shown you my shepherd's heart, as your mother-in-law served us last week instead of us burying her, and your coffers are currently filled with fish.

Jesus's call to follow is our call, too. It's a purpose for each of us. Follow. Rely on him. Let him guide. Change directions when necessary. Let go of certain boats. Trust in the face of uncertainty.

Follow.

It took two chapters to get here, but here we are. We follow. But we're also called to help others follow, and herein lies a problem, because where Jesus was the perfect rabbi and leader, we aren't.

Give a human a little power, and sometimes he wants more. Put a man in charge, and things can go wrong.

Our final chapter happened on Jesus's final night before his crucifixion. It was a beautiful command and warning, because if we try to disciple one another, we will fail unless we keep one more purpose in mind.

It's a simple one in theory. But it might be more difficult to put into practice than simply becoming a martyr, Peter's go-to claim for how much he loved Jesus. It's harder than fishing for men and catching them alive.

Our next stop on the road to purpose and significance requires humility and selflessness, and to acquiesce to this purpose is almost as important as accepting that first call to follow.

Next we head to an upper room for Passover, where we lose our shoes and let Jesus wash our feet.

Clean Feet

I've suggested every Christian's main purpose, his very reason for walking the road, is to build the kingdom through discipleship. This includes being a disciple, calling others to be disciples, and actively training disciples.

We do this with God-given authority. We take aspects of Jesus's role of rabbi with one another, the goal being life transformation.

I used a piece of this quote earlier, but now I'm going to share more of it, because this so beautifully demonstrates the disciple mindset. The author begins by explaining that we in the West think of discipleship as an education, but the Eastern view is much truer.

The Eastern view encompasses the understanding that Jesus died for our sins and that belonging to him involves repenting and receiving him as Lord. But it also recognizes that Jesus lived transparently in front of his disciples in order to teach them how to live. They, in turn, were to live transparently before others, humbly teaching them the way of Christ. This approach involves not just information but transformation. God's goal isn't simply to fill the world with people who believe the right things. It is to fill the world with people who shine with the brilliance of Christ.[1]

We touched on all three aspects of discipleship earlier—being, calling, and training—but now we look at a story of Jesus that includes both a lesson and a warning.

Why a warning? Because Jesus gave his disciples authority. That means power. And what do people do with power? We mess everything up. I imagine you can instantly come up with one name—likely more than one name—of a human leader in your life who leads with arrogance and pride. You probably have a harder time naming one who doesn't.

For this lesson we have stepped off the road. Jesus has called people for three years. Some stay with him as full-time followers. Some open their homes when he comes through town. Others were sent home to live for Jesus there. Now we get to Jesus's final days, and he speaks to his inner circle. They have no idea that within a few weeks they will be Jesus's voice in this world. And with that great responsibility in mind, he gives them an uncomfortable, awkward lesson.

Let's look at John 13:1-17. Because it's long, we'll just take the first part here.

The evening meal was in progress, and the devil had already prompted Judas, the son of Simon Iscariot, to betray Jesus. Jesus knew that the Father had put all things under his power, and that he had come from God and was returning to God; so he got up from the meal, took off his outer clothing, and wrapped a towel around his waist. After that, he poured water into a basin and began to wash his disciples' feet, drying them with the towel that was wrapped around him. John 13:2-5

This happened on or the day before Passover. A few days earlier Jesus journeyed to Jerusalem, where he was anointed with perfume by Mary and greeted with a crowd that threw palm branches and cloaks on the ground. Then, according to John 12:36, Jesus hid himself from the crowds for a few days.

Maybe he hid because the main event is about to start, and this event required some quiet preparation, either with God, with the disciples, or both. John makes it clear this final event starts before the cross. It starts here in this upper room with his disciples, where, according to John 13:1, Jesus *fully loved them* or *loved them to the end*, depending on your translation. The whole of the crucifixion includes these moments beforehand where he teaches his final lessons.

At this important and fancy meal, Jesus suddenly rises, strips off his outer cloak, and wraps a towel around his waist. I imagine the room gets silent. This is not normal feast activity. Eyebrows rise. Some start to squirm. Jesus is doing it again, not quite acting like a normal rabbi.

Look at two things we know about this moment. First, Jesus

knows Judas is about to betray him. What happens next, this moment of humble servanthood, isn't limited to the eleven who trust Jesus. He lavishes this care on one who will set in motion the most abominable event in history.

N.T. Wright points out *The power of darkness is closing in, but Jesus is meeting it with love, and even joy.*[2] Jesus is fully aware of the weight of these final moments. Nothing that will happen in next few hours takes him by surprise. And yet this is how he chooses to spend those hours, caring for his people, even one who doesn't care for him back.

Second, Jesus fully knows the score here. He has authority over all things. He is God's son, and he is about to head back to live in Heaven with his Father. Knowing that about himself, he kneels at the feet of his people and washes their feet.

This isn't about a rabbi doing the unthinkable. It's much bigger than that. And by saying it this way, John demolishes any excuse I might ever give for backing away from service. Do I have all authority? Did I come from the Father? Um, no. Then if Jesus can serve this way, so can I.

Never, ever, ever

If you've spent any time in church, you know the background of ancient Israel and dirty feet. First, they would be dusty, not necessarily filthy. Jerusalem would be kept as clean as possible for the crowds coming for Passover, the same way we spruce up our houses for guests.

However, dirty feet are dirty feet, and the second thing to know is that in this culture, nobody wanted to clean them. This was a job for a servant, a wife, or a child. And not just any servant. The job was usually held for a foreign servant.

When Jesus took the basin and rag and walked to the outside of the circle of disciples, kneeling at one's feet and removing his sandals, the disciples were shocked. Maybe a little disgusted. Definitely uncomfortable. It's no surprise Peter fought this. Touching a leper to heal him is one thing, but to crouch in the posture of a foreign slave is something else altogether.

We read it this way:

He came to Simon Peter, who said to him, "Lord, are you going to wash my feet?"
⁷ Jesus replied, "You do not realize now what I am doing, but later you will understand."
⁸ "No," said Peter, "you shall never wash my feet."
Jesus answered, "Unless I wash you, you have no part with me."
⁹ "Then, Lord," Simon Peter replied, "not just my feet but my hands and my head as well!" John 13:6-9

This is an uncomfortable, awkward moment. I imagine more than one disciple was tempted to pull his feet up under his robe and not let Jesus touch them. Peter might be the one who spoke up, but no doubt all of them were thinking similar thoughts.

According to author Kenneth Bailey, who studies the Bible in light of Middle Eastern culture, there are no other stories about rabbis serving in this way. No anecdotes exist where a rabbi stoops to this level of servanthood.[3] The humility of the act is almost lost in its social intolerability.

To put it simply, one commentator suggests Peter's denial here is more along the lines of *You will not in all eternity wash my feet.* Never, ever, ever.

They didn't like this one bit.

Then Peter, upon hearing how important this is to Jesus and what it can mean to his future as a disciple, completely changes gears. If washing is required, he's ready to offer his head and hands for further cleaning.

I'm pretty sure Jesus smiled at the words. Maybe rolled his eyes.

Jesus uses this moment to teach them about the need to be diligent in cleaning off the influences and sins of the world, but that's a side bar to our story. Important, of course, but better left for another discussion.

We step back into the story in verse 12:

When he had finished washing their feet, he put on his clothes and returned to his place. "Do you understand what I have done for you?" he asked them. *¹³ "You call me 'Teacher' and 'Lord,' and rightly so, for that is what I am. ¹⁴ Now that I, your Lord and Teacher, have washed your feet, you also should wash one another's feet. ¹⁵ I have set you an example that you should do as I have done for you. ¹⁶ Very truly I tell you, no servant is greater than his master, nor is a messenger greater than the one who sent him. ¹⁷ Now that you know these things, you will be blessed if you do them.* John 13:12-17

First, he puts his clothes on and returns to his place. He is still Jesus, and he still sits at the head of the table. Object lesson is over, and the debriefing is about to begin.

I wonder at what point the disciples stopped staring wide-eyed at Jesus. He just suggested they take on the lowest job ever, and they do it for one another. Did Peter look at his brother and grimace? Who wants to wash his brother's feet? Did each of them glance into the face of the man across from him and then take another glance at that person's feet? This was a little much to swallow.

Beyond feet

I'm sure they realized this wasn't about feet. They knew what Jesus was saying. Touching lepers, talking to untouchable women at wells, now doing the lowliest jobs for one another—Jesus asked a lot of them.

It was one thing for a disciple to serve his master. That was expected. Jesus asked them to serve everyone, even those who were far, far down the social ladder.

What did Jesus say would be the result of doing this? Blessings. Living out this command resulted in blessing.

Why did Jesus make such a bold, memorable, awkward lesson on his final day? I think we can look ahead at centuries of church history and see why. Many, many church leaders throughout the ages didn't pay attention to this command. Leaders throughout history have used their authority to be served and not to serve. They became the shepherds of Isaiah, who scattered the sheep and left them for wolves instead of gathering them for blessings.

Jesus knew the hearts of men, and this call to be a servant was a dramatic warning.

It's a warning that still stands today.

I love reading the books of *Peter* in light of the gospels. We see that Peter takes everything Jesus said to him to heart. After telling church leaders and young parishioners how to behave toward one another, Peter says in 1 Peter 5:5 *All of you, clothe yourselves with humility toward one another, because, "God opposes the proud but shows favor to the humble."*

And in 1 Peter 3:8: *Finally, all of you, be like-minded, be sympathetic, love one another, be compassionate and humble.*

History tells us Peter lived this out to the end, dying a martyr's death for Jesus's sake. He didn't send someone beneath him to die. No, he faced the end himself. Like Jesus, a suffering servant to the end.

Many of us find ourselves in leadership positions in the church, in a job, in a family, as a parent. The warning stands for all of us, as does the promise of blessing for the humble leader. Peter, Paul, and the rest of the epistle writers say the same, that we are to serve instead of being served. This keeps us from the sins of entitlement and arrogance that shipwreck the church on the egos of proud men.

Seen and Invited

This is our last chance to imagine what Jesus saw and our last chance to explore Jesus's invitations, so let's do it well.

What he saw that evening was sobering. He saw men who loved him deeply. Let's never doubt that. Except that one who would betray him. That one must have broken his heart, because he clearly saw that, too.

Those who loved him broke his heart, as well, because he sees men who are about to get scared, doubt him, and flee. Jesus's closest people are about to abandon him during the darkest moments of any person's life in the history of this world. How painful that had to be. What he saw must have ached down to his very vulnerable, human bones.

He sees their futures, though. He sees men who will humbly return, men he will forgive. He sees them journey forward in a dangerous world, and he sees most of them succumb to martyr's deaths, painful and scary. Again, his heart aches. He loves them deeply, and that will lead them to difficult places. Oh, the horrors of life in a sinful world for a man determined to rescue it.

> The invitations of discipleship are very simple. Come. See. Follow. Serve.

He sees even further to you and me, who will benefit from the preaching and teaching and discipleship of these men. That part brought him joy, all the faces in the future that depended on the events of the next few hours for their eternal salvation.

And the invitation?

Serve. The invitations of discipleship are very simple. *Come. See. Follow. Serve.*

With a simple vocabulary we have a recipe for a lifetime of wonder. Not one of those things comes easily. Each requires help from the Spirit, the influence of a godly community, and time in the Word. Each of them requires constant travel with the Shepherd along the roads, journeying together to the end.

They are easy to say, simple words a child understands. But living them out takes a lifetime and includes me, the ones who teach me, and those who will learn from me. It's a chain started two thousand years ago that hasn't ever broken and never will break. The enemy has tried and will continue to try, but never will that chain falter.

Disciples will make disciples until the end.

So in our discipleship invitation, *serve* is this final word.

But it's not serving in simple ways. Serve by crouching in front of dirty feet. Serve those who don't think they're worthy of the sacrifice. Serve those who might betray you.

Serve real needs. We skipped the discussion about baths and cleansing, but the important point there is that all of us pick up dirt from the world, and all of us are to help the others clean that off. We warn one another. We look out for one another. When the need arises, we wrap in a towel and crouch.

That crouched position… How often have we seen that in these stories? Jesus has now taken both sides, but whichever side you're on, there's a moment of connection. At that moment both participants see one another, and for a moment that's all they see.

Beautiful bunions

I don't think this passage was a call to begin a discipline of foot washing. However, I don't think there's anything wrong with occasionally acting out this moment in Jesus's history.

I once had the opportunity to join a Maundy Thursday worship service that included washing feet. And it's awkward from both sides. Crouching at someone's feet to wash them is humbling. But at the same time, it's a job that can be done well. That gives you something to focus on. Wash. Dry. It has steps and direction.

I found the other side to be more awkward. Having someone wash my feet was just as humbling as washing, which is why I think the disciples wanted to pull their feet up and not let it happen. I sort of felt that myself.

We don't always know how to serve, nor do we know how to be served. Discipleship calls us to do both. Jesus offered help and asked for help. So will I.

In my fiction writer persona, I wrote a book about a character who attends church barefoot to remind himself that on Sunday he stands in the presence of God—on holy ground like Moses. At the end of the book, after many dramatic moments, the pastor stages an impromptu foot-washing ceremony before worship. The congregation finds chairs and basins inside the doors, and they are encouraged to wash feet or let someone else wash their feet before entering the sanctuary.

One old woman says she can't possibly do this, because she has a bunion, and that's not attractive. To which the main character responds *God says the feet of those who bring good news are beautiful. And you take the good news outside these walls every week, so I think that means you have beautiful feet.*[4]

I think that's the attitude we need with one another. That's the attitude Jesus wanted from his men. We don't look at the bunions or the scars or the lint between someone's toes. We look at the beauty. Jesus looked into the eyes of the blind and saw beauty. He touched the skin of the leper and felt hope. And we face one another's dusty, misshapen, bunion-covered feet and see lambs Jesus loves. We clean off the dirt with a smile and step back onto the road, ready for the next steps. And when our feet need washed, we settle in that chair and let someone help us.

Jesus spends a lot of time warning about those who abuse and misuse power. The warning is for leaders of the world, leaders within the church, and for each of us. We are to be disciples. We use the skills God gives us to build up the body, each of us living transparently among the others as we wrestle each day to live in light of God's love and his commands.

But if we took this one story to heart, and we stooped at the feet of our fellow followers, carefully and lovingly washing off the dirt of the world, cleaning off the grit that makes our sandals chafe, and drying those feet so they can take the next steps cool and comfortable and healthy, we would shine for the world. Wasn't that what writer Ann Spangler imagined the goal to be?

Nothing stands out like a group of people that cares so much for one another they will set all social expectations aside and move from love alone.

The heart of the story

We don't get to discuss at length the next part of the story, when the Shepherd lays down his life for the sheep, when every lesson comes to fruition and every recipient of his love and healing suddenly sees their moments with the rabbi in a new light.

That moment is where all this was heading. It's what we look back to as we take every step on our own roads. It's what the men of old looked ahead to see.

Because that moment colors all the rest, I can't write a book on Jesus without a reminder that his sacrifice, his death, gives life to everything else he did. It also happened on a dusty road in sight of the crowds, but it was nothing like anything else in his life. Or in anyone's life.

Remember at the beginning of this book, when I mentioned Jesus could have stood in front of a city, raised his arms, called thunder, and healed everyone at once? Here at the cross, after three years of shepherding his people, that's what he did.

And it didn't look like anyone would imagine. The kingly blessing that could lead to healing and prosperity for his people was raw and bloodied and humble. Were his arms raised? Yes. Was there thunder? Yes. Was there healing? Oh, yes, yes, yes.

But as always, Jesus didn't give us what we expected. Instead, he gave us what we needed. He stooped to the lowest level, lower than a crouch at dirty feet, and secured that cleansing Peter asked for. He secured the forgiveness he spent years promising to the lost on the road. He secured our future community and our purpose, and he fulfilled the conditions for the sending of the Spirit to walk with us on every road through the end of time. Only because of his death and resurrection could he be with us forever. Without these moments in time there would be no roads at all.

The hands that touched the broken were punctured. The shoulders that held so many lambs scraped harsh wood in agony, bleeding and torn. The blessing of the king came in gasping breaths and, while encompassing the world, still took in each lamb, offering forgiveness to his executioners, promises to a thief, and provision for his mother.

Because to the end, he was the Shepherd. He may return three days later the victorious king, but he still cooks breakfast. Jesus is still and always Jesus.

That's what his Spirit brings to mind, and it's what we should share with one another to keep us centered on the right road. So let's end with a moment to remember that all of this led to the cross, and every moment afterward leads back to the cross.

You and I work to create a new kingdom. The centerpiece of that kingdom is a king who came down in humility to woo us to him. He could have demanded homage. He could have used fear and anger to force our allegiance. Kings do that all the time.

But he chose humility in life and humility in death to love, heal, woo, satisfy, connect, and send us. First of all, though, that humility forgave and rescued us.

Now we step forward and live that out.

You are seen. Whatever road you're trapped on, Jesus sees you and wants to call you back to a better road.

You are invited. You have purpose. You matter, and the kingdom depends on you doing what Jesus has set for you to do.

But whatever you are called to do, you will do it in the framework of humble discipleship, following the humble rabbi, the selfless Shepherd, the Lamb of God.

Into the Future

We touched a lot in these pages. Many books exist on each of these topics: healing, discipleship, fulfillment, community, and purpose. Most of them do it much more completely than I did here.

But I want you to take the first steps toward a new road. Whatever trips you up, whatever keeps you from embracing Jesus fully—face those things in light of the Shepherd who seeks you as a lost lamb. Face them in light of a rabbi who does nothing expected because he will go to any lengths to speak to a harassed crowd.

Jesus came to die. But before that he came to show us God. The God of the Old Testament is the same God who touches lepers and spits on blind men. He's the same God willing to crouch at our feet—is the crucifixion anything less than a drop into intolerably humble servanthood?—and jump to quell our fears. He's the same God who longs for us to live in communion, knowing it's not right for us to live alone.

Jesus offers healing and reminds us that healing is about more than our bodies. It's about our hearts and our souls.

Jesus shows us his power and authority to keep us from living in fear and doubt, because fear and doubt derail many of us and leave us in the ditches at the sides of these roads.

Jesus knows our deepest needs and seeks to satisfy and fulfill all of them. He alone knows the inner workings and desires of his creation, and he alone has answers to give us direction and contentment.

Jesus knows we are created for community. And because human community is a mess, he spent years here living within it as a beacon of how it's to be done, with humility and tenderness for each person within each community.

Finally, Jesus gave us a purpose. He wants us to do as he did. He taught that purpose in words, showed us in actions, and then sent us the Spirit to make sure we got it. Discipleship is our goal, to see it and live it in every relationship, both relationships with men and that with God.

Every morning you step onto the roads. I hope you see Jesus today beckoning you forward on the roads that lead to life.

We're building a kingdom, one that will last forever. I'm glad you're here to build with me.

A Note from Jill

If this book spoke to you, would you consider helping spread the word? Just like Jesus moved from individual to individual, this book will be doing the same. To help it along, please consider leaving a review (Amazon, Goodreads, Bookbub, etc.). Share it on your favorite social media platform. Suggest it to church ministry leaders.

Or, pass a copy along to a friend. I'd love to see old, worn copies make the rounds until they fall apart. It's not about making money or selling a lot of books. Writing this book changed my relationship with God more than anything has in decades. I want to see it do the same for many, many more people—what a blessing it would be to stand at Jesus's side and help him gather more and more lambs!

Blessings and thank you!

--Jill

Jill@JillPenrod.com

Study Guide

This study guide is useful for both personal study and group studies. The book lends itself well to a six-week study, tackling the introduction one week, and then one section per week after that, which includes three to four chapters.

If using in a group, the following tips and thoughts might be helpful.

*Time per week: Allow 75-90 minutes for each group meeting

*Possible meeting schedule:
1. Open with prayer.
2. During the first week, make time for introductions if the group doesn't know one another well.
3. You may or may not choose to introduce the main points from each week's reading.
4. Start discussion time by opening the floor for anyone to mention insights or comments they have about the week's readings. Spirit-prompted conversations always trump book questions.
5. Pick and choose questions from each chapter. End with one or more of the group questions for each section.
6. Some of the questions are very personal, especially the *To Start* questions. Know the comfort level of your group before using those. If you need to stick with the less personal questions, do that. Use these questions as a buffet, and take and leave what you will.
7. Because this book deals with weakness and brokenness, some participants will want to turn this into a counseling session. While sharing is good, this isn't the place to solve someone's problems. Be ready to steer the discussion back to the topic and offer to find help outside the session time for anyone who

needs it.
8. Close with a clear explanation of what to read for next week, and send the group off with prayer.

The Journey Begins

***Main points**: Our view of Jesus evolves over time and because of our circumstances. We need to know why we think the way we do and then use Scripture to know the truth about Jesus.

1. How do you see Jesus? How would you describe your relationship with him? What do you want your relationship with Jesus to look like?
2. On page 11, Jill describes Jesus's balancing act while he was here. What does this refer to?
3. The introduction follows the path of Jill's relationship with Jesus. What does your journey with Jesus look like? What events in your life color your relationship with Jesus?

***Group Questions**: The three questions above tend to fill the time with no other group questions needed.

The Road of Brokenness

***Main points**: Jesus came to heal broken lives. He healed physical ailments, but he never stopped there. His goal was to heal spirits and souls and gather lambs for the kingdom.

Proximity Matters: Being close to Jesus is the first step to wholeness.

Do You Want to Get Well?: As Jesus heals our lives, we are capable of doing more and bigger jobs in the kingdom.

The Touch of the Shepherd's Hand: Jesus inserted his human, physical body into his encounters. He was all in. We, too, can expect His touch in our lives through the Spirit, and we are called to get close

Study Guide

to those around us.

True Wholeness: Jesus didn't stop at fixing outward circumstances. He was interested in healing entire lives.

*To Start: Do you see yourself on this road? If so, name specific areas you want to see healed and made whole.

Proximity Matters
Luke 5:18-28
1. What was the condition of Israel when Jesus came onto the scene? Consider their politics, spiritual life, and economy.
2. Why was Jesus's forgiveness unimpressive to the people in the house? What was the reality behind the claim?
3. Wholeness doesn't always mean physical healing. So what does it mean?
4. What was Jesus's invitation in this story?
5. What does it mean that proximity matters? How can you get closer to Jesus? How can you help someone else get closer to Jesus?
6. Some verses to consider: Psalm 73:23-28; Psalm 84; James 4:8

Do you Want to get Well?
John 5:1-15
1. According to Genesis 2:15, what was our pre-sin purpose? What did sin to do this purpose?
2. Again, do we learn anything more about wholeness in this chapter?
3. When Jesus heals a broken part of your life, what might change for you? What new responsibilities might wholeness bring?
4. Verses to consider: Psalm 90:17; Ephesians 2:10; Ephesians 4:11-13.

The Touch of the Shepherd's Hand
Mark 1:40-45; 7:32-36; 8:22-26
1. Biblically, what were the four purposes of touch? (p 33)
2. Look at Isaiah 35:5-6. (p 36) How is Jesus living out these prophesies?
3. What might have been the lesson in Jesus's partial healing of the blind man in Mark 8:22-26?
4. What were some of the cultural problems with Jesus using touch to heal a leper?
5. Are there areas of your life that need Jesus's personal, healing touch? Areas that other people shun or areas you wish to cover up?
6. How can you welcome the Spirit to touch and heal your untouchable places? Do you recall a time the Spirit did this for you?
7. Verses to consider: Genesis 48:12-16; 2 Timothy 1:5-7

True Wholeness
John 1:1-41
1. How does the blind man's understanding of Jesus's identity change as this story progresses?
2. Why does Jesus return to the blind man? What does this man still need?
3. Jesus asks the man *Do you believe*? Spend time with that question. How does the blind man answer? How would you answer? What is the deeper invitation in the question?
4. Jill suggests true wholeness results in worship. Does this mirror your experience? Should it?
5. Verses to consider: Matthew 16:13-16; Psalm 139:7-12

*Group questions: The Bible doesn't use the term *wholeness*. Based on these readings, what might wholeness mean? Do you agree that Jesus desires to make his people whole?

The Road of Doubt and Fear

***Main Points**: God knows we fear and doubt. Jesus spent time tenderly quieting and calming both fears and doubts as he drew them close.

Sunk by Doubt: Jesus calms a storm to teach the disciples both His power over the world and His concern and care for them.

I Do Believe: If we are honest with Jesus about our fears and doubts, He responds in love, not anger.

Incomplete Faith: Even if we have little faith, Jesus honors that and will use it to mature us. We don't need to wait until we have it all together to come to Him.

***To Start**: What are some of your doubts and fears concerning Jesus and living for him? How do doubt and fear affect your relationship with Jesus?

Sunk by Doubt
Matthew 14:28-33; Mark 6:47-50

1. Jesus didn't rescue his disciples immediately. Why might he have waited?
2. When Jesus got to the men, what did he do first? (p. 53) What might this say about Jesus's feelings toward our fears?
3. Why might Peter have wanted to get out of the boat to walk with Jesus? What does Jesus's response to Peter's request say about his feelings on this water walk?
4. Why did Peter sink? How did Jesus respond? How will Jesus respond to your fear and doubt?
5. Jesus asked Peter why he doubted. If Jesus asked you this question, how would you respond?
6. What was Peter's invitation from Jesus? Is this invitation for you, too? How will you respond?
7. Verses to consider: Psalm 40:1-3

I Do Believe
Mark 9:14-29
1. At the beginning of this reading, what Old Testament event had Jesus reenacted?
2. Who are the main players in this story? How does Jesus interact with each of them?
3. How does Jesus respond to the father's honest assessment of his faith? How will Jesus respond to your honest admission of doubt or fear?
4. What might Jesus mean when he says everything is possible for one who believes?
5. What were Jesus's invitations in this passage?
6. Again, why do you doubt? Take the answers straight to God.
7. Verses to consider: Psalm 40:11-13; James 1:2-6

Incomplete Faith
Mark 5:21-43
1. Describe the two people Jesus deals with in this passage.
2. What led the woman to hide her desire from Jesus? How does he respond to her deception?
3. Why might Jesus have healed one of these in public and the other in private?
4. What were Jesus's invitations to these people? How does this relate to your life and your faith?
5. Verses to consider: Psalm 25:1-2; John 14:1-2

***Group Questions**: The main players in this section are the Disciples, Peter, the father, and the bleeding woman. For each of these, determine what they feared or doubted, how Jesus responded to this fear and doubt, and what invitations he issued. End with the personal questions *What do you fear or doubt concerning Jesus? What invitation might Jesus have for you?*

The Road of Discontentment

*Main Points: Jesus knows us better than anyone, so He knows what fulfills us. Also, He cares about our contentment and satisfaction.

In Need of a Drink: The woman at the well needed fulfillment in her relationships. Jesus also wants us to have fulfilling relationships with Him and with one another.

Filled Baskets: Jesus cares for our physical needs, and we ought to care for one another's physical needs, as well.

Delighted by Understanding: Jesus doesn't demand blind obedience. He shares with us and wants us to understand Him. Curiosity is a God-given trait.

*To Start: Where do you seek satisfaction and contentment? What does the Bible say about satisfaction?

In Need of a Drink

John 4:4-42
1. In what areas of her life is the Samaritan woman unfulfilled?
2. What steps or questions does Jesus use to draw this woman to him?
3. In what ways is Jesus's discourse with this woman similar to a marriage proposal?
4. What holes existed in this woman's life, and how did Jesus fill them? What holes exist in your life, and how can Jesus fill those?
5. What makes a relationship with Jesus different from a relationship with anyone else?
6. Verses to consider: Psalm 63:1-8; Revelations 7:16-17

Filled Baskets and Mother Love

Mark 6:3-44; 8:1-9
1. What convinced Jesus to set aside his plan to rest with the disciples and instead serve five thousand people dinner?

2. What Old Testament stories did Jesus bring to mind with this miracle?
3. How did the first crowd respond to this feast?
4. What might the three days in Jesus's presence have looked like for the second crowd?
5. What was Jesus's invitation to the crowds, either directly or indirectly? Does this invitation mean anything personally to you?
6. Verses to consider: 2 Kings 4:42-43; John 6:32-40; Acts 14:16-17

Delighted by Understanding
Luke 24:13-35
1. What is the context of this passage?
2. Why might Jesus have hidden his identity?
3. Why is it important to understand God's kingdom before we can advance it?
4. What was Jesus's invitation in this passage?
5. What is the role of the Spirit in our understanding of spiritual truths?
6. Describe the relationship between knowledge, understanding, and delight.
7. Verses to consider: Amos 4:13; Colossians 2:2-3; John 14:26-27

Group questions: How might our lives look different if we sought satisfaction in God and not in the world? How might this change the church as a whole?

The Road of Isolation

Main Points: We are made to live in community. Jesus healed many people by restoring them to their community, and He modeled healthy community.

No Strength of Her Own: Some people are outside community

through no fault of their own. Jesus restored these people, and we should also look for those who don't fit and pull them into our community.

When the Crowd Won't Forgive: The crowd didn't understand Jesus calling Zacchaeus. We should embrace those who repent of sin and want to return to the fold.

Restoration After a Fall: After Jesus's resurrection, the disciples—and Peter in particular—needed assurance they were forgiven and restored in Jesus's eyes. Jesus gives them what they need to grow and move on.

*To Start: What are the dangers of being isolated without community? How would you assess the role of Christian community in your life right now?

No Strength of Her Own
Luke 7:11-17
1. Describe the two crowds who met in this story.
2. At the beginning of the story, what did the widow's life look like? What did it look like at the end?
3. What Old Testament events did Jesus reenact here? (p. 121) What did this convey to the crowd?
4. What were Jesus's invitations in this story?
5. Jill tells a story about God speaking to her through a borrowed bell. (p. 122) Do you have any *borrowed bell* stories of your own?
6. What can you do to lead those on the edges back to the safety of community?
7. Verses to consider: Psalm 107:4-9; Acts 42-47; John 13:34-35

When the Crowd Won't Forgive
Luke 19:1-10
1. What might have led Zacchaeus into that tree?
2. How did the crowd respond to Jesus inviting himself to Zacchaeus's house for dinner?

3. Jesus dealt with two lost souls in succession, a blind man and then a tax collector. Why did the crowd react so differently to the two events?
4. What are Jesus's invitations in this story?
5. Do you see yourself in Zacchaeus? In the crowd? Have you been shunned or shunned others for past sins? What can you do about either situation?
6. Verses to consider: Matthew 6:14-15; Colossians 3:12-14

Restoration After a Fall

John 21

1. What might these disciples have been doing together in Galilee? What can we infer about their relationship when this story opens?
2. When Jesus appears, what does he do for the disciples? Why might he have done these things?
3. Why might Peter have needed special words of restoration here?
4. What were Jesus's invitations in this passage? How might these invitations relate to your life?
5. Verses to consider: 1 John 3:19-24

Group questions: Based on these readings and your experience, what does a healthy Christian community look like? What can you do to encourage spiritual community in your church or among your people?

The Road of Insignificance

Main Points: We are called into discipleship. We are to *be* disciples, *make* disciples, and *train* disciples.

Come and See: Jesus approaches each person differently, seeing that person clearly, to make a discipleship call.

Gone Fishin': When Jesus asks people to follow him, he asks for their whole lives. He also cares for our whole lives.

Clean Feet: Humble servanthood is the posture of a mature Christian disciple.

*To Start: What makes the quest for purpose so important? What would you claim as your life purpose? Or your purpose for this season of your life?

Come and See

Mark 1:16-17; John 1:35-51

1. What does Jill posit as the universal purpose/activity for the Christian?
2. Describe how Jesus called Andrew and his friend. Peter. Nathaniel. What can we infer about Jesus's means of calling people from these events?
3. What is Jesus's invitation in this passage?
4. How is a person called to discipleship today?
5. What role can you play in the calling of disciples? What limits do you have?
6. Verses to consider: Matthew 28:16-20; John 17:20-24

Gone Fishin'

Luke 5:1-11

1. What favor does Jesus ask of Peter? What is Peter's reward for his obedience? What is Peter's response to Jesus's miracle?
2. What mission or purpose did Jesus give the group at this point?
3. Why might Jesus have punctuated his call to full-time discipleship with a miracle?
4. What is Jesus's invitation here? Include the words and the deeper implications.
5. How can you respond to this invitation?
6. Verses to consider: Matthew 10:37-39; John 10:27-29

Clean Feet

John 13:1-17

1. What does Jesus do for his disciples in this passage? How did the disciples respond? Why did they respond this way?
2. What warning was implied in Jesus's actions? What are the dangers when people ignore this lesson?
3. What was Jesus's invitation here?
4. Jill tells a story of beautiful bunions (p. 172). What attitude does this suggest we take toward others and ourselves?
5. What are some practical ways you can live out this chapter?
6. How did Jesus fulfill his role of shepherd even in the midst of the crucifixion?
7. Verses to consider: Psalm 25:4-10; Philippians 2:1-4; 1 Peter 5:2-3

Into the Future...

1. Did any one road stand out to you? Do you have any concrete ideas about moving from the wrong roads to the right?
2. Just to recap: Jesus wishes to move us from the *Road of Brokenness* to the *Road of* _____. The *Road of Doubt and Fear* to the *Road of* _____. The *Road of Discontentment* to the *Road of* _____. The *Road of Isolation* to the *Road of* _____. The *Road of Insignificance* to the *Road of* _____.

***Group Questions**: Discipleship can be broken into several single-word invitations. How do we live those out? If we aren't discipled by Jesus, are we still being discipled by other things? Finally, finish with the *Into the Future* question and give everyone a chance for a final comment on anything in the book that spoke to them.

Notes

Do You Want to Get Well?
1. Jeremiah 17:22 does say not to carry a load into Jerusalem or out of one's house on the sabbath. *The Expositor's Bible Commentary (Abridged Edition): Old Testament*, as quoted on Biblegateway.com, says this passage refers to carrying loads to be sold or in preparation for the work week, as was the common practice. When Jeremiah wrote this, the Sabbath was regularly used to bring in harvests and set up for commerce the next day, which was what Jeremiah spoke against.

The Touch of the Shepherd's Hand
1. Keener, Craig. *The IVP Bible Background Commentary: New Testament*. Illinois, Intervarsity Press. 1993. p 156

True Wholeness
1. *Expositor's Bible Commentary*, as quoted by BibleGateway.Com

Sunk by Doubt
1. *Matthew Henry's Commentary* via Biblegateway.com
2. Matthew Henry
3. Wiersbe, Warren. *Warren Wiersbe BE Bible Study Series*. David C. Cook. 2007

I Do Believe
1. Garland, David. *NIV Application Commentary*, 1996. 592
2. Wilmhurst, Steven. *A Ransom for Many: the Gospel of Mark Simply Explained* (Welwyn Commentary Series); © 2011 EP Books.
3. Wilmhurst, Steven.

An Incomplete Faith

1. Bailey, Kenneth E. *Jesus Through Middle Eastern Eyes: Cultural Studies in the Bible.* Illinois, Intervarsity Press, 2008. 14

In Need of a Drink

1 Bailey, Kenneth E. 204
2 Bailey, Kenneth E. 215
3 Terkeurst, Lysa. *Good Boundaries and Goodbyes.* Thomas Nelson, 2022
4 MacDonald, William. *The Bible Believer's Commentary* via BibleGateway.com

Filled Baskets and Mother Love

1 Mark 6:34 *Orthodox Jewish Bible*, Copyright © 2002, 2003, 2008, 2010, 2011 by Artists for Israel International as presented on BibleGateway.com

Restoration after a Fall

1 *IVP New Testament Commentary Series* via Biblegateway.com

Come and See

1 TheSowerMagazine.com/the-calling-of-the-disciples/
2 *Expositor's Bible Commentary* via Biblegateway.com

Gone Fishin'

1 Bailey, Kenneth E. 140
2 Bailey, Kenneth E. 142
3 Keener, Craig. 201
4 *IVP New Testament Commentary Series* via Biblegateway.com
5 Spangler, Ann and Lois Tverberg. *Sitting at the Feet of Rabbi Jesus: How the Jewishness of Jesus can Transform your Faith.* Zondervan, 2018. 60

Clean Feet

1 Spangler, Ann. 69

2 Wright, NT. *The New Testament in its World*. Michigan, Zondervan Academic, 2019. 673

3 Bailey, Kenneth E. 373

4 Penrod, Jill. *The Barefoot Bard*. Kentucky. 2023. 200

With Gratitude...

I need to say a special thank you to my family, who let me disappear into this book for the better part of a year. It wasn't what I'd planned to write, and it took time I wasn't expecting to spend.

I also need to thank my dear new friend Therese, who turned out to be this book's biggest cheerleader, as well as all the beta readers who gave me pointers along the way.

Another special shout-out goes to Pastor Rick Durrance, whose sermon got this whole thing started and whose encouragement along the way kept me moving forward.

Words cannot describe what I owe the small group who let me try this book and the study guide out on them. They were gracious, encouraging, and gave me the final push to present this book to the world.

Finally, a thank-you to a pair of ladies I've never met. Louis Tverberg and Ann Spangler, who wrote *Sitting at the Feet of Rabbi Jesus...* When I read that book, Jesus began to fill out in all his dimensions in a way he never had before. I am forever grateful.

Jesus, you know all these thanks pale in comparison to the gratitude I feel for you for showing up and wooing me close this year. What an amazing journey!! I pray, Jesus, you and the Spirit will use these words to woo countless others close in the future.